The Gift is Given

In December 1943 Dr Tom Honeyman (1891–1971), Director of the Glasgow Art Galleries, received a surprise phone call. It was Sir William Burrell (1861–1958), wealthy Glaswegian shipping magnate, businessman, and respected art collector. From the late 1880s, William Burrell, initially on his own and then with his wife Constance, Lady Burrell (1875–1961) had acquired an extraordinary art collection bought with the profits from his shipping company, Burrell & Son. This vast hoard eventually included medieval tapestries, ivory, wood, alabaster sculpture, Chinese ceramics, Islamic carpets, stained glass, furniture and paintings. Over the decades, pieces decorated the various Burrell family homes, including Hutton Castle in the Scottish Borders.

Burrell asked Honeyman to make a secret visit to Hutton. With no indication of what was to be discussed, Honeyman made his way by train. At the castle, Sir William revealed that he and his wife were gifting their entire collection to the City of Glasgow.

Honeyman was so excited he could barely speak.[1] It would be one of the greatest gifts the city had ever received.

The exhibition, *The Burrells' Legacy: A Great Gift to Glasgow*, tells the story of the formation of the Burrell Collection, from a private art collection to a civic museum. Over 100 magnificent objects from the Collection help to reveal the dedicated efforts of William and Constance, the Glasgow Corporation, architects and other key players, to find and create a permanent home to house the magnificent collection in its entirety. This book focuses on highlight objects from the exhibition, demonstrating the vast breadth and scale of a collection that has inspired the people of Glasgow from its initial donation in 1944 to its refurbishment and redisplay over 75 years later. *The Burrells' Legacy: A Great Gift to Glasgow* celebrates the Collection of Sir William and Constance, Lady Burrell, which has brought international recognition to their native city.

[1] ART AND AUDACITY: Dr T. J. Honeyman, STV Dateline, Scottish Television (1971).

Making a Museum Collection

The Collection was officially donated in May 1944, with an additional £450,000 given to build a museum to house and display it. Sir William Burrell was a shrewd businessman, bringing this expertise to the amassing of his collection. He meticulously detailed in his own hand every purchase from 1911 to 1957 in 28 school exercise books. A knowledgeable, determined collector; strong-willed, with a reputation for haggling with dealers, he managed to snap up stellar bargains and valuable pieces during his 75 years of collecting. This collection was his life-long passion, and it came as no surprise that Burrell's involvement continued after the gift. He had an instrumental role, organizing the moving of the Collection from Berwickshire to Glasgow. He also continued to purchase objects for the Collection.

These acquisitions were decisive purchases, designed to enhance existing areas of the Collection. Around 2,000 objects were bought post-1944. At first, Burrell continued to purchase objects using his own finances, donating items to the Collection, but after 1949 he gained permission to buy objects on behalf of the Glasgow Corporation, using the interest from his financial donation of £450,000 to fund these purchases.[2] Burrell consulted with reputed dealers and art historians to expand and vet his collection, including Perceval Yetts (1878–1957), first Professor of Chinese Art and Archaeology at London University, and an expert in Chinese bronzes. Yetts was invited to Glasgow in 1948 to check the ancient bronzes. Except for two pieces, quickly sold on by Burrell, Yetts approved all Burrell's bronzes. Rigorous checking of the Collection was necessary to make sure the objects were good quality and to certify Burrell's reputation as a collector now that his personal collection was to be in the spotlight on a national and international stage.

[2] Richard Marks, *Burrell: A Portrait of a Collector*, Richard Drew Publishing (1988), p.180.

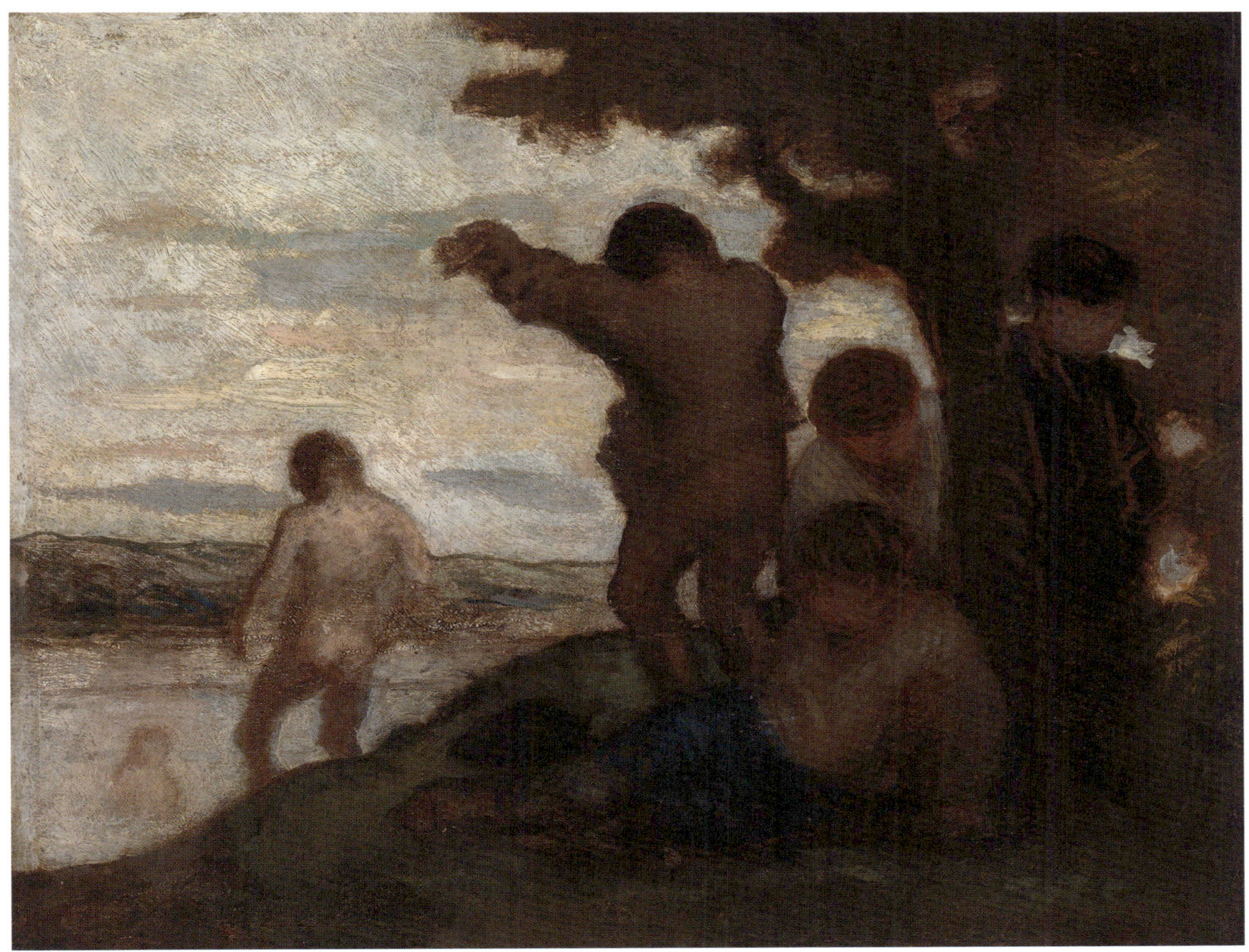

By the late 1800s, French art was growing in popularity with Scottish collectors. Burrell was an early collector, buying through trusted art dealers, often from the collections of his fellow wealthy Glasgow industrialist collectors.

Burrell purchased this painting in 1936 from prominent Glasgow art dealer Alexander Reid (1854–1928). It was previously owned by A. J. Kirkpatrick (d. 1900), a Glaswegian collector and chemical merchant, and

The Bathers, about 1846–48
Honoré Daumier
Oil on panel
25.4 cm x 32.1 cm
35.212

is one of a series of paintings of bathers by Daumier made between 1846–48. It shows boys undressing to bathe in the River Seine in Paris; one boy struggles to get out of his large shirt.

Burrell started collecting Chinese art in the early 1900s, establishing an extraordinary collection of ceramics from the Neolithic Period (7000–200 BC) to the Qing Dynasty (1644–1911). He managed to acquire several rare and fine examples of Ming porcelain, known for its distinctive cobalt-blue and white colour. This large porcelain jar is decorated with flower scrolls, flaming pearls and a water scene of waves, rocks, and seaweed, and two five-clawed dragons.

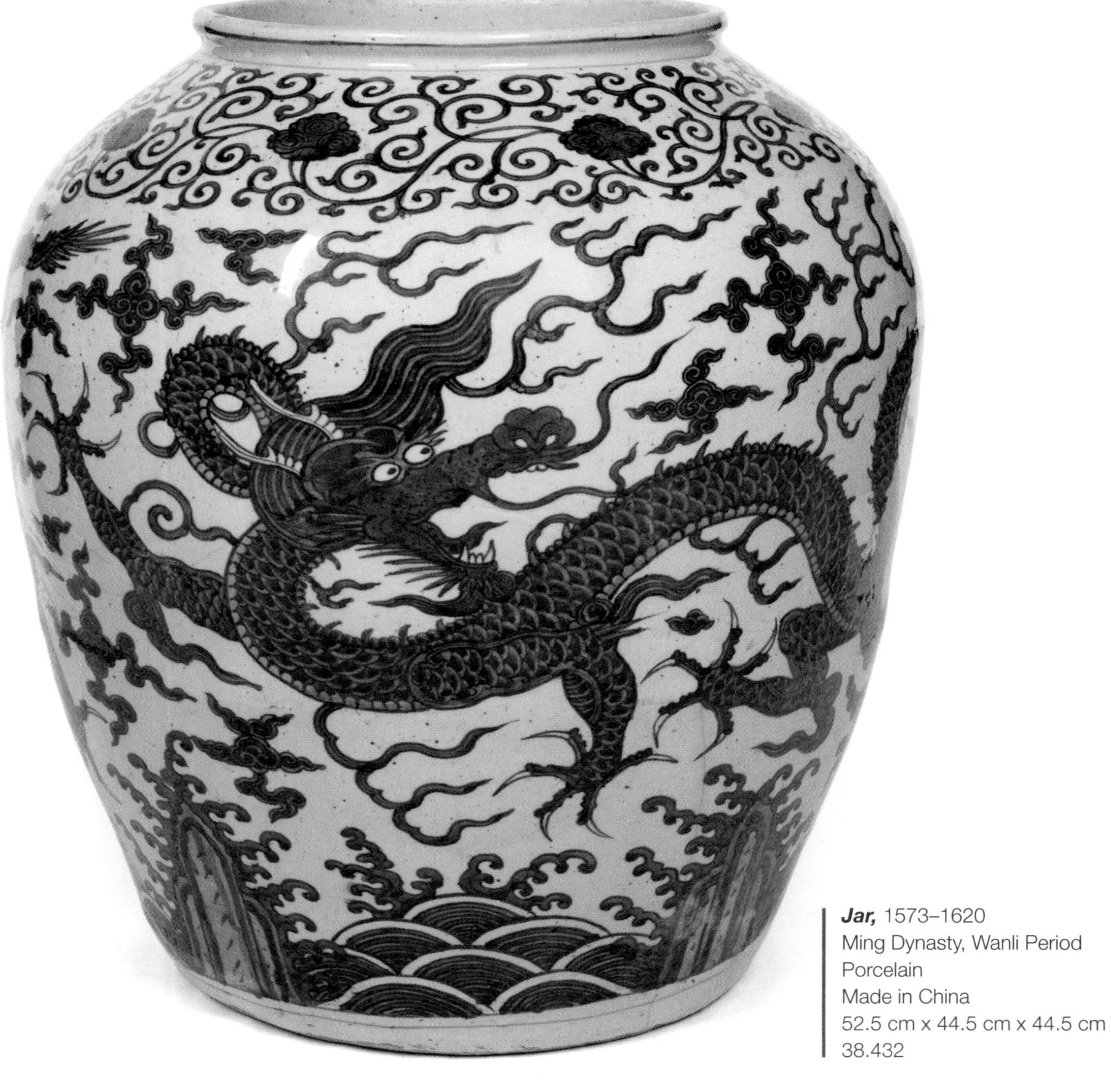

Jar, 1573–1620
Ming Dynasty, Wanli Period
Porcelain
Made in China
52.5 cm x 44.5 cm x 44.5 cm
38.432

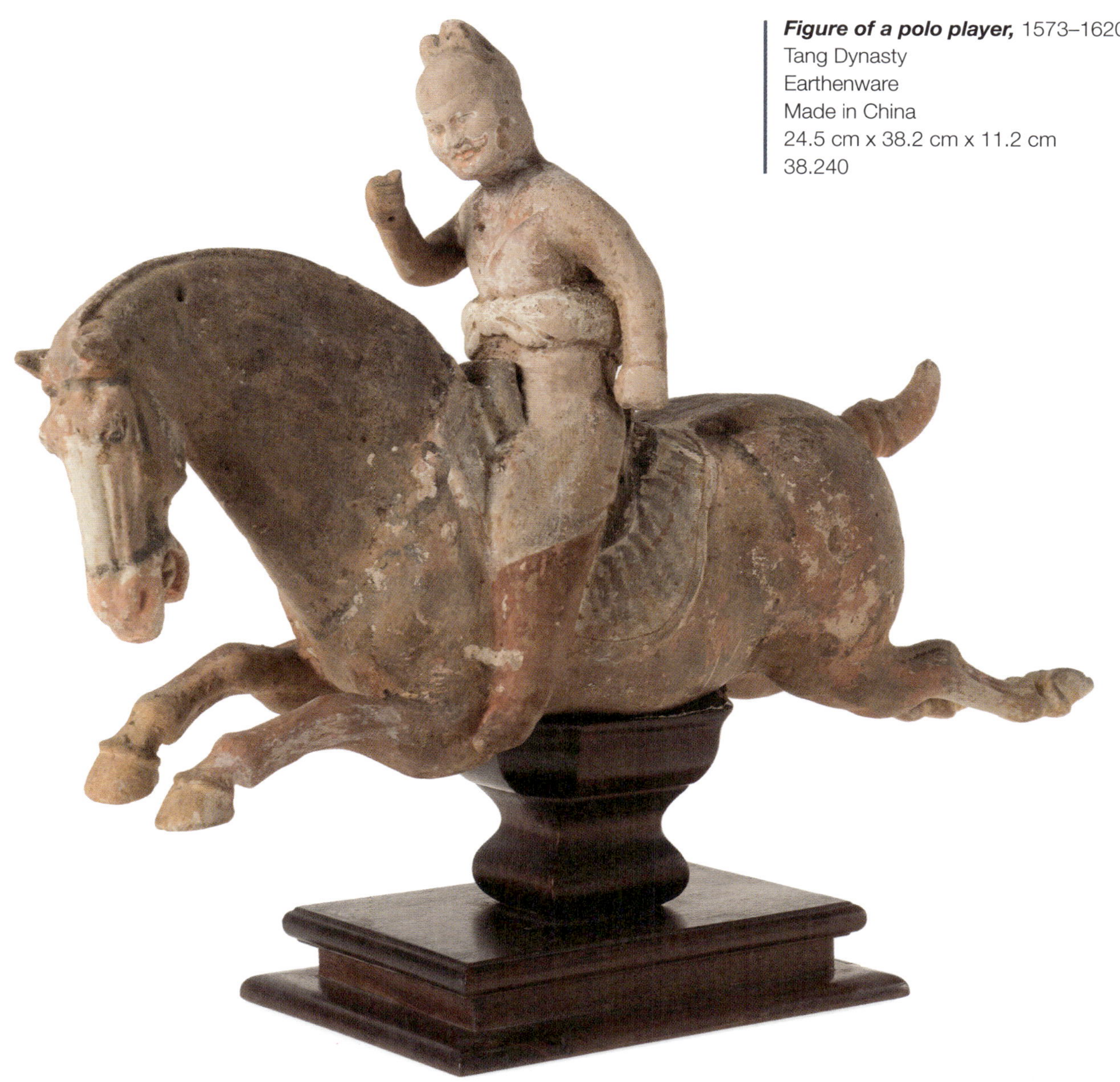

Figure of a polo player, 1573–1620
Tang Dynasty
Earthenware
Made in China
24.5 cm x 38.2 cm x 11.2 cm
38.240

Burrell's purchases post-1944 included larger, figural tomb ware of the Han, Tang, Song, and early Ming dynasties. Wealthy people from these periods were often buried with tomb ware representing commodities required for the leisure pursuits they would undertake in the afterlife. Tang Dynasty tombs often contained figures of polo players, like this figure acquired in 1954. Polo was a popular sport for both men and women of the Tang Dynasty courts. Burrell's polo player is possibly a woman, her horse's muscular legs flying out as it gallops through the game.

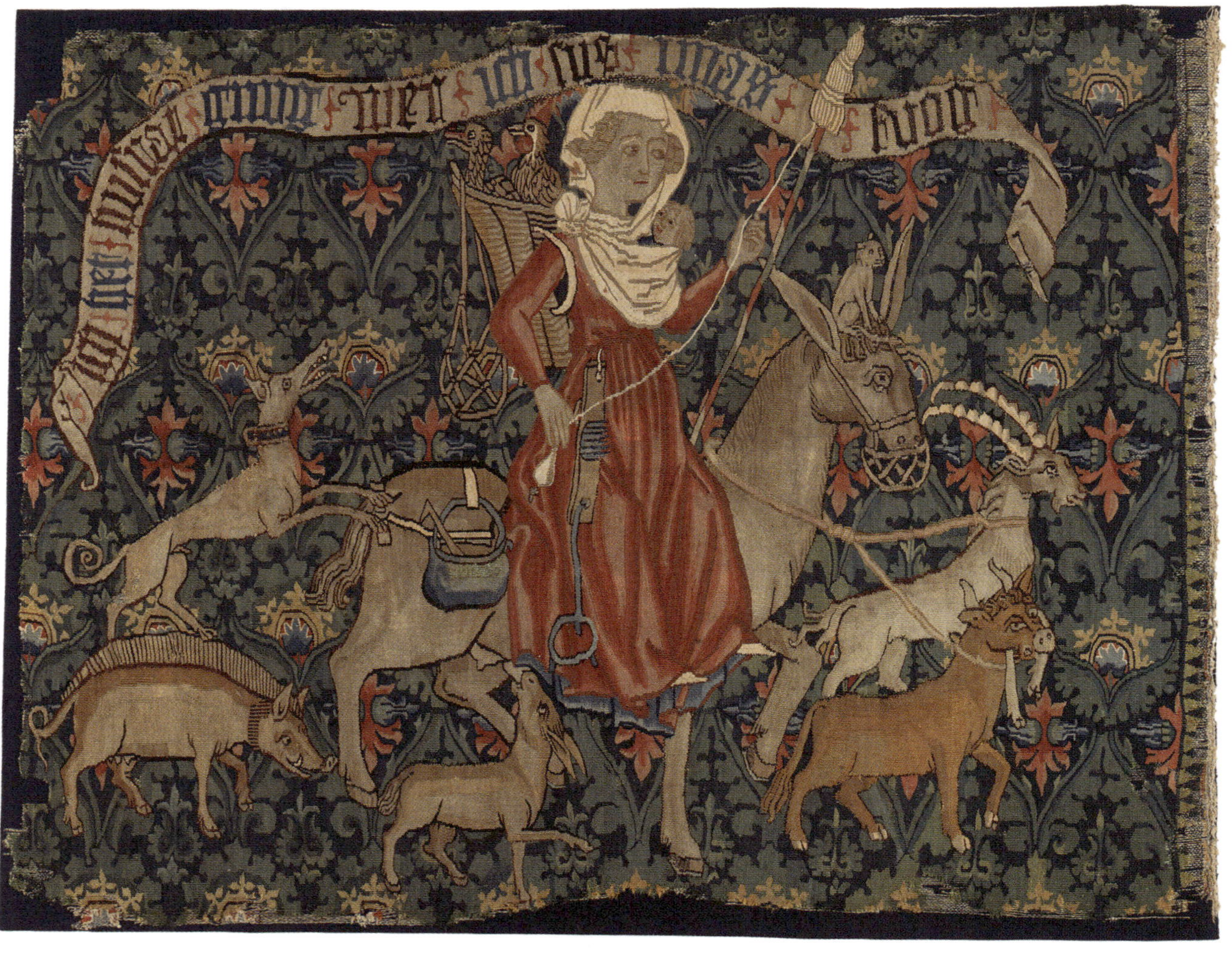

The Wandering Housewife, about 1470–80
Linen, wool, metal
Made in Switzerland
86 cm x 109 cm
46.39

William Burrell considered his medieval tapestries to be the most important part of the collection. In 1943, Glasgow Corporation hired Dr Betty Kurth (1878–1948), a historian of German medieval art, to research and write a catalogue of the tapestries.

In 1939, Kurth had been forced to emigrate to London from her home in Vienna to escape the persecution of the German Nazi Party in Austria. Burrell's catalogue was an important and welcome commission. Kurth brought new insights to the Collection. For example, she suggested that this tapestry, showing a busy female figure surrounded by animals and household belongings, would have been understood in the 1400s as a criticism of overenthusiastic, self-important housewives, showing off their domestic skills.

Collecting the Ancients

Prior to the 1944 donation, Burrell had rarely collected objects from ancient civilizations. To make sure the Collection was more representative of a worldwide history, Burrell focused his attention on these purchases. Between 1944 and 1957, the largest number of acquisitions were objects from Mesopotamia (modern-day Iraq, Kuwait, Turkey and Syria), Egypt, Greece, and Rome, Italy.

Due to the necessity of this rapid expansion Burrell did not have the opportunity to personally check each object before purchase, as was his habit. Instead, objects were acquired straight from dealers, and Burrell checked their condition through photographs. He also referred to books from his personal library of over 1,000 volumes, to expand his knowledge of ancient civilizations. He extensively annotated the pages in ink or pencil with his personal notes. Many ancient civilization history books in Burrell's library contain such annotations, revealing his continued engagement with his collection even in the later stages of his life. The library was added to the Collection in 1961, following the death of Constance, Lady Burrell.

As part of his Roman collection, William Burrell bought this fragment of mosaic, showing a proud cockerel, in 1954. The floors of public buildings and houses owned by wealthy Romans were often decorated with mosaics made of tiny tiles, known as tesserae, stuck together with cement or plaster to create pictures of everyday life with humans and animals. Once part of a much larger mosaic floor, this fragment uses colourful cubes of tile to create the cockerel, with golden wings and long green tail feathers.

Mosaic fragment of a cockerel, 100 BC–0 AD
Stone, plaster
Made in Italy
32 cm x 36.7 cm x 3.2 cm
42.3

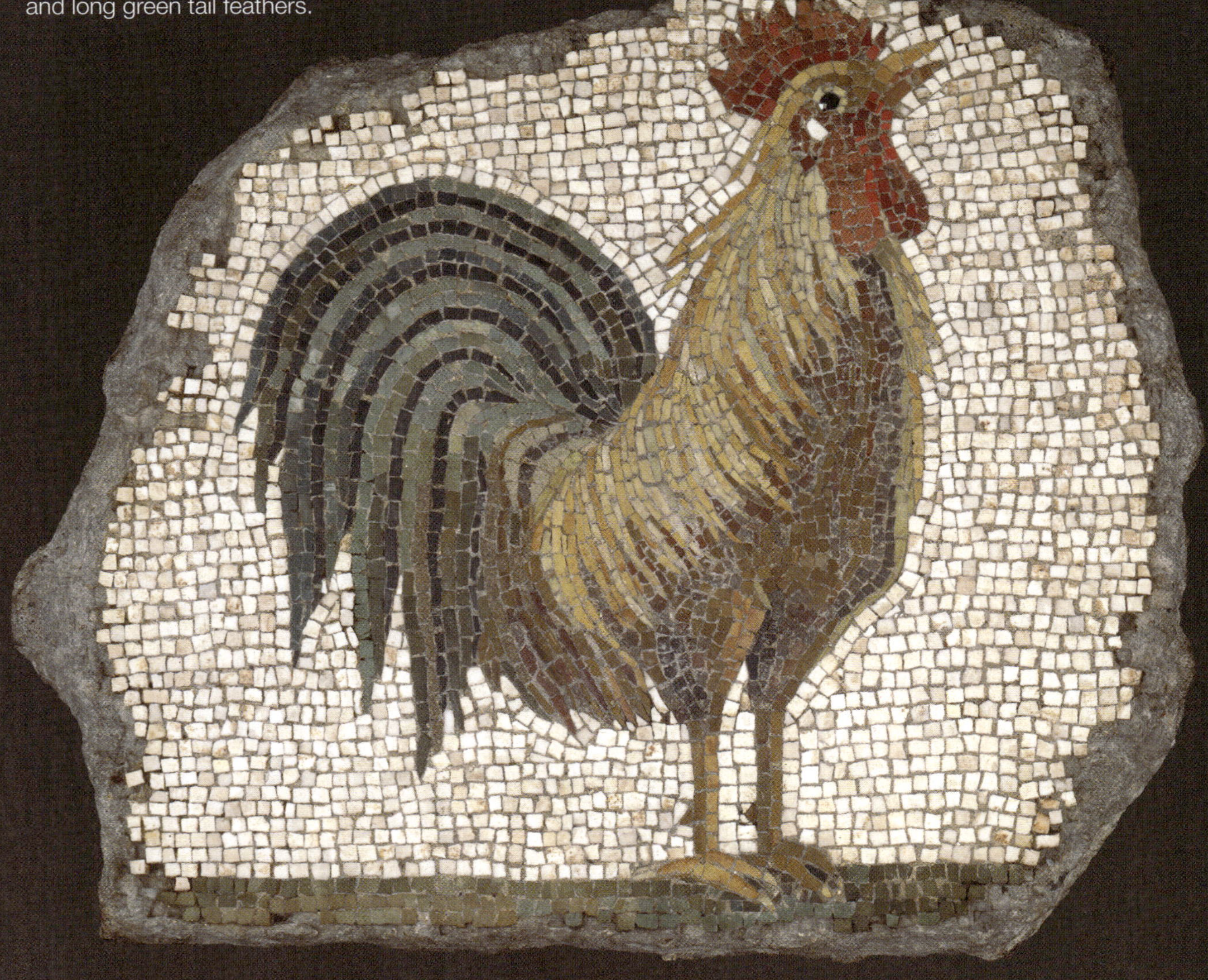

William Burrell had only purchased four Ancient Egyptian objects before 1944. From 1947, he increased this number to over 300. One of the most significant purchases, a gilt ibis mummy case, was made in 1955. The mummification of animals was a popular practice in Egypt. Ibis were sacred birds, understood as a representation of Thoth, god of learning. Thousands of Ibis were mummified and placed in cases, like this one, as a gift to honour Thoth.

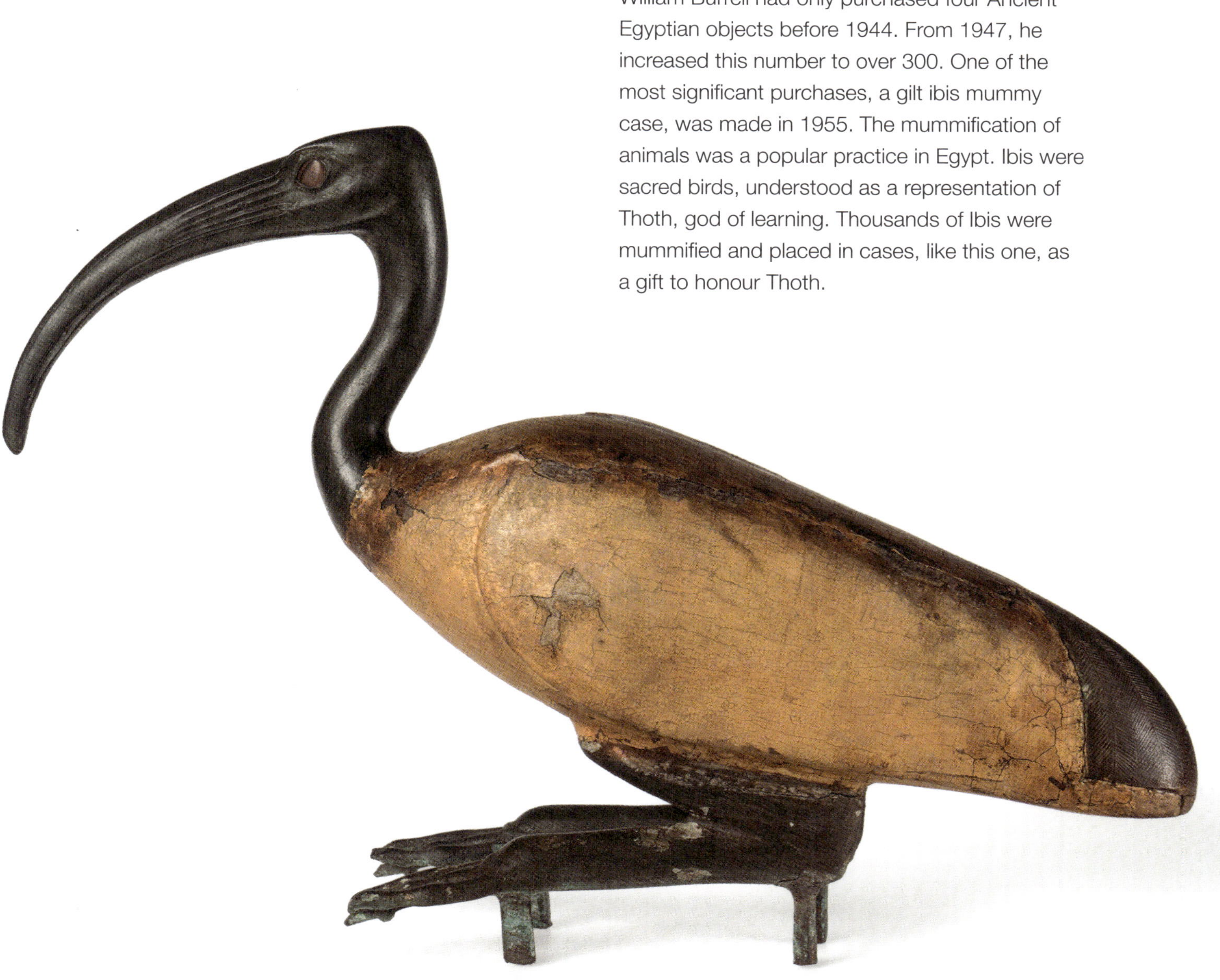

Ibis mummy case, 332–30 BC
Ptolemaic Period
Wood, bronze, glass, gold
Made in Egypt
32.8 cm x 46.4 cm x 12 cm
13.283

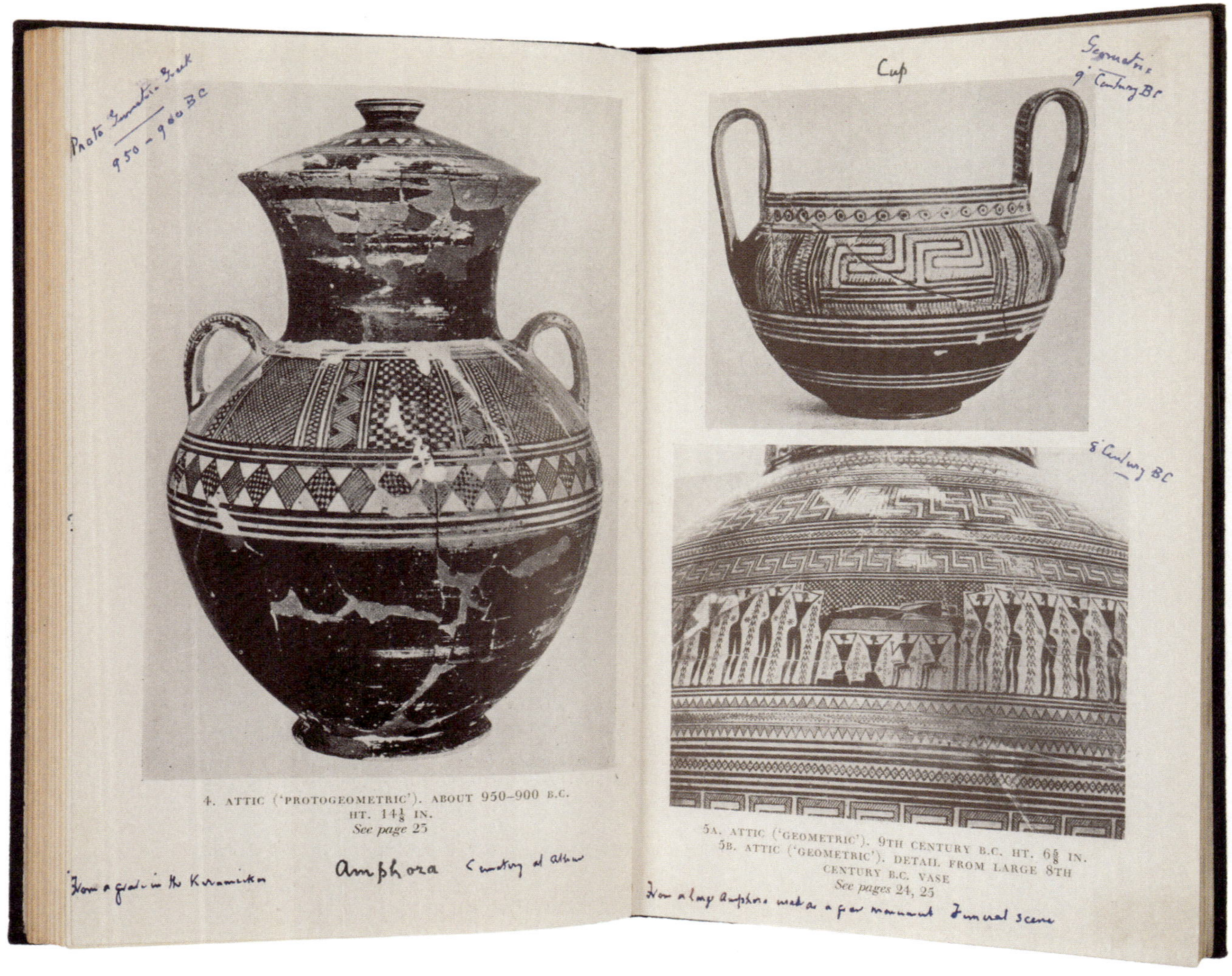

Greek Pottery was published in 1948, so Burrell probably bought his copy around this time when he was also acquiring Greek objects. Burrell wrote notes on nearly every page, and on the inside back cover he composed his own quick-reference guide to the styles and shapes of Greek pottery and their domestic uses.

Greek Pottery, 1948
Arthur Lane
Published by Faber & Faber
Paper, ink, cloth
25.3 cm x 16 cm x 2 cm
GMA.2013.1.6.3

This two-handled amphora was bought the same year *Greek Pottery* was published. Amphorae were often used for the storage of wine or olive oil. This one is decorated in the Attic black-figure technique. Decorative figures were painted with a slip in silhouette on the unfired clay vase. Once fired, the slip turned black. Details were then incised, allowing the orange colour of the clay to show through. The decoration includes a four-horse chariot and its charioteer on one side; on the other, the Athenian hero, Theseus, killing the Minotaur, a creature half-man, half-bull.

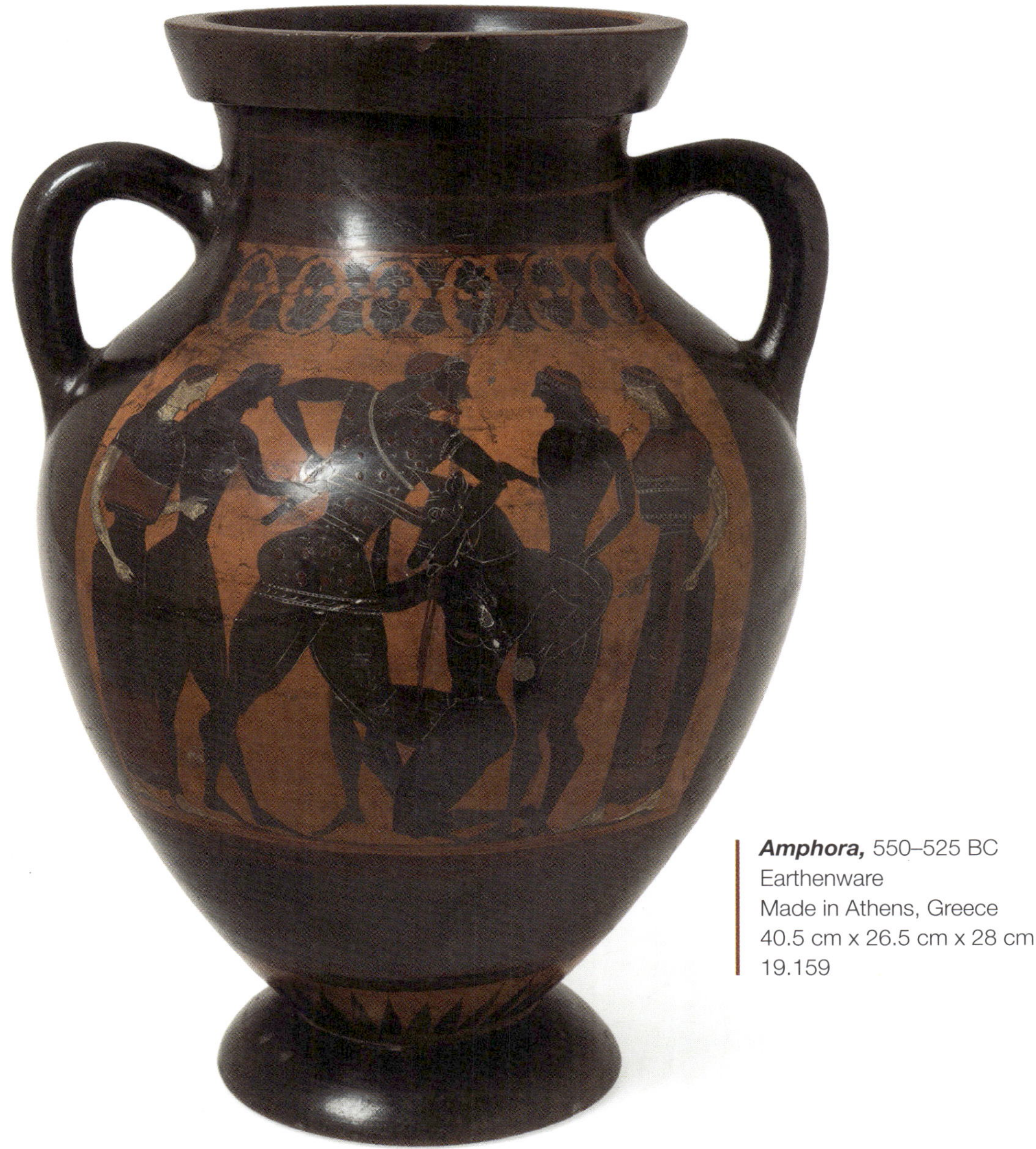

Amphora, 550–525 BC
Earthenware
Made in Athens, Greece
40.5 cm x 26.5 cm x 28 cm
19.159

Burrell collected ancient Mesopotamian objects, from the areas of Iraq and Iran, representing the Sumerian, Assyrian, and Babylonian periods. This carved head is a fragment of a worshipper statue. The statue would have been placed in a temple as a votive representation of the individual worshipper who owned it, giving them a continuous presence in the temple. The body of the worshipper statue has been lost.

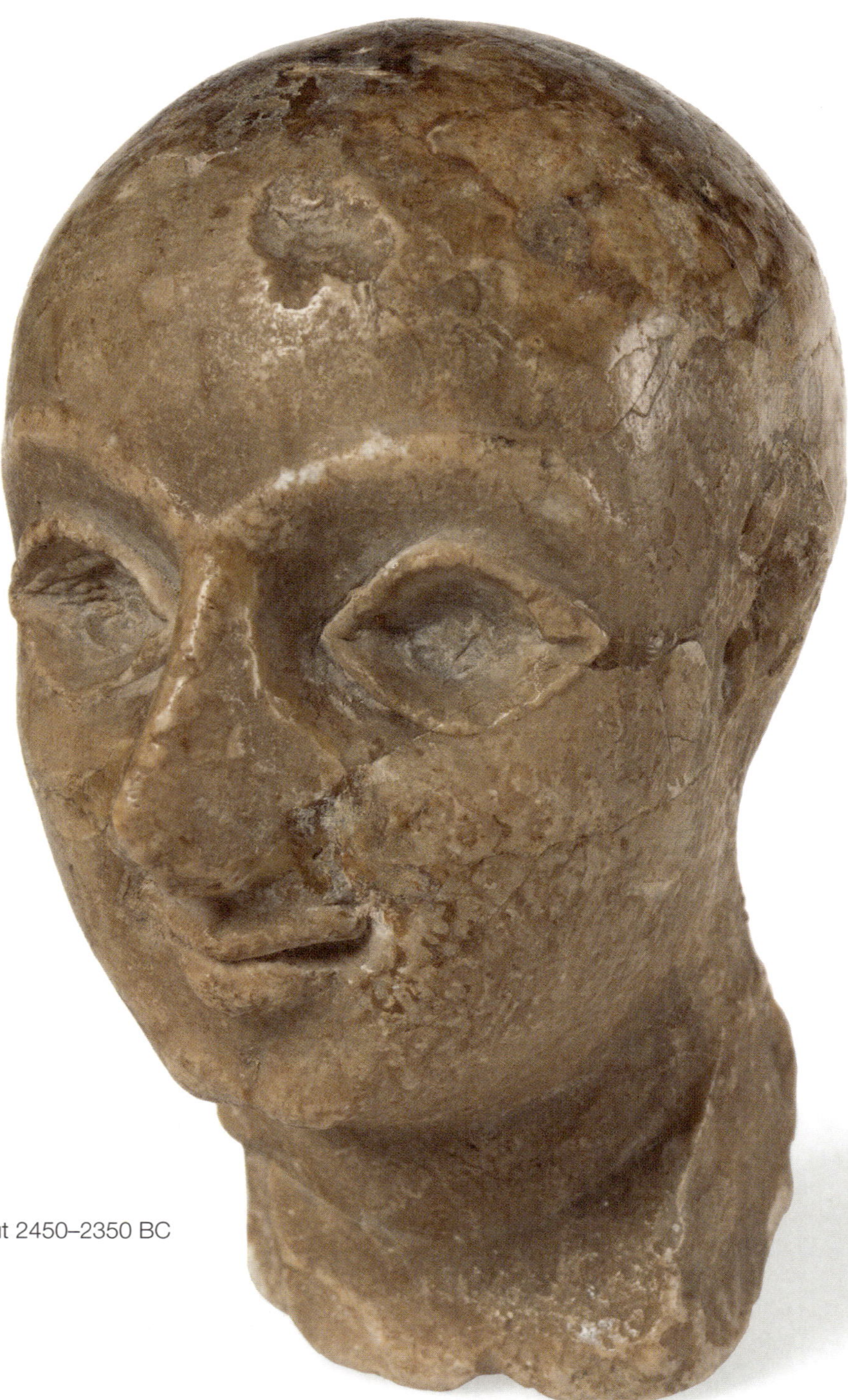

Head of a worshipper statue, about 2450–2350 BC
Early Dynastic III period
Limestone
Made in Iraq
13 cm x 6.9 cm x 9.1 cm
28.5

First Looks at the Collection

During the 1940s and 1950s objects were gradually removed from Hutton Castle and stored in various sites across Glasgow while a permanent home for the Collection was sought. Aikenhead House, in King's Park, sheltered most of the Chinese art and furniture collection. From 1963, objects were also housed at the former Coplawhill Glasgow Corporation Tramways depot, on Albert Drive, in the south side of the city.

Exhibitions of the Collection were held in 1946 and 1951 at the Kelvingrove Art Galleries to celebrate the donation. In 1949, a summer exhibition of over 1,000 objects opened in the McLellan Galleries on Sauchiehall Street, in Glasgow city centre. This was the first time the people of Glasgow were able to see the overwhelming breadth of Burrell's collection. Entry was free to all on a Friday[3], and newspaper reports from the time recommended visitors 'would be wise not to try to cope with it all at once'[4], and instead purchase a season ticket to revisit.

It was the first time Burrell would have seen his collection in the one place. He had a personal hand in the organization of the exhibition, visiting the weekend before opening to oversee final arrangements. Spread over nine galleries, the exhibition showed selections of Chinese porcelain, furniture, ancient civilizations, Islamic carpets, medieval tapestries, and embroideries. The fragile textiles were only included because it was a temporary exhibition; Burrell had stipulated with the Deed of Gift that the Collection must be permanently housed in a rural setting at least 16 miles from Glasgow centre, protecting the tapestries and textiles from the city's air pollution, which was rife at the time.

[3] *The Scotsman*, 11 June 1949.
[4] *The Scotsman*, 11 June 1949.

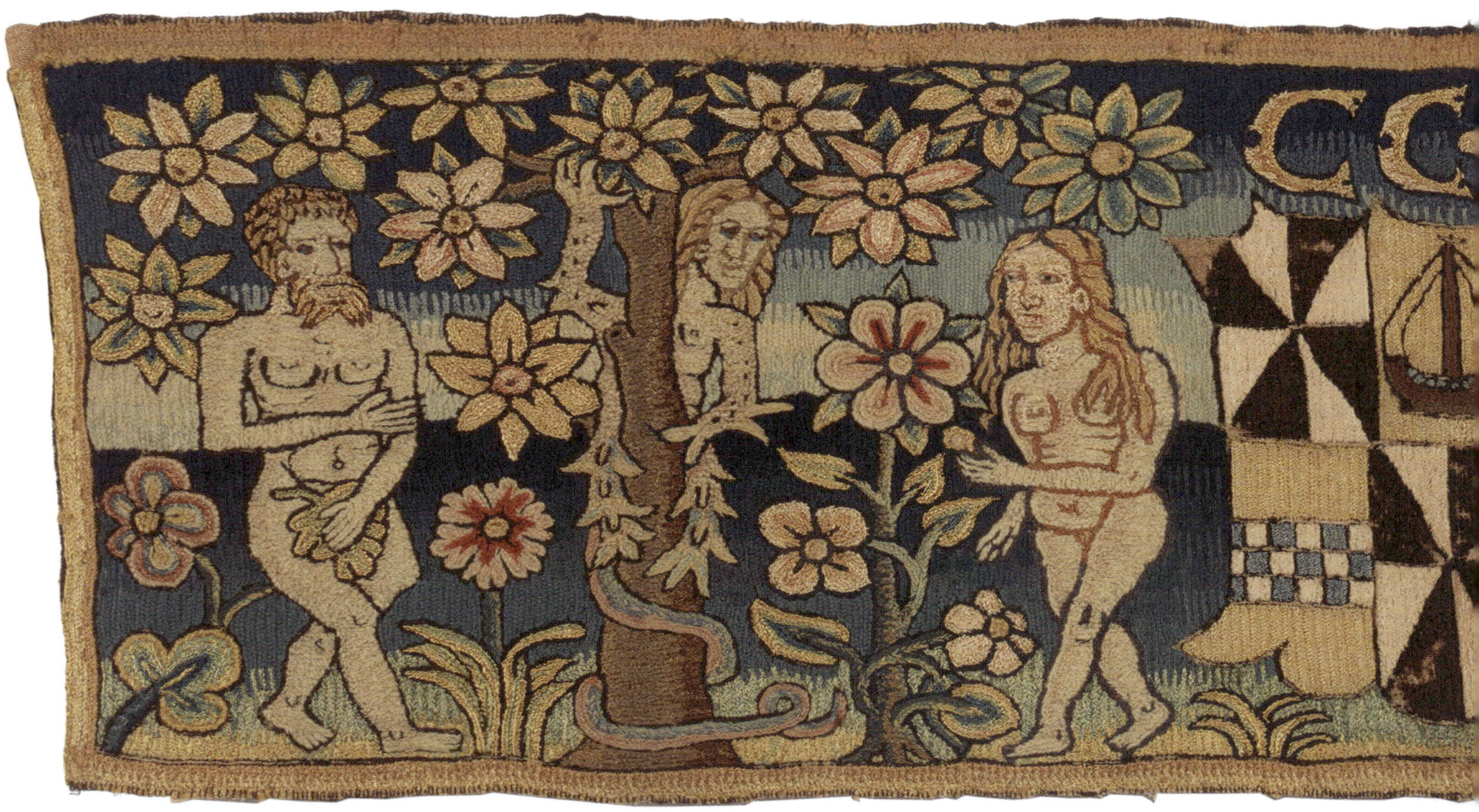

This valance is one of a set of three made for Sir Colin Campbell of Glenorchy (1499–1583), possibly to commemorate his marriage to his second wife Katherine Ruthven (d. 1583–84). Purchased in 1933, these may be the earliest surviving set of Scottish valances. The valance is embroidered with scenes from the biblical Book of Genesis, including the Temptation of Adam and Eve, and the Expulsion from the Garden of Eden. The centre is embroidered with the initials of the married couple 'CC' and 'KR', above their conjoined coat of arms.

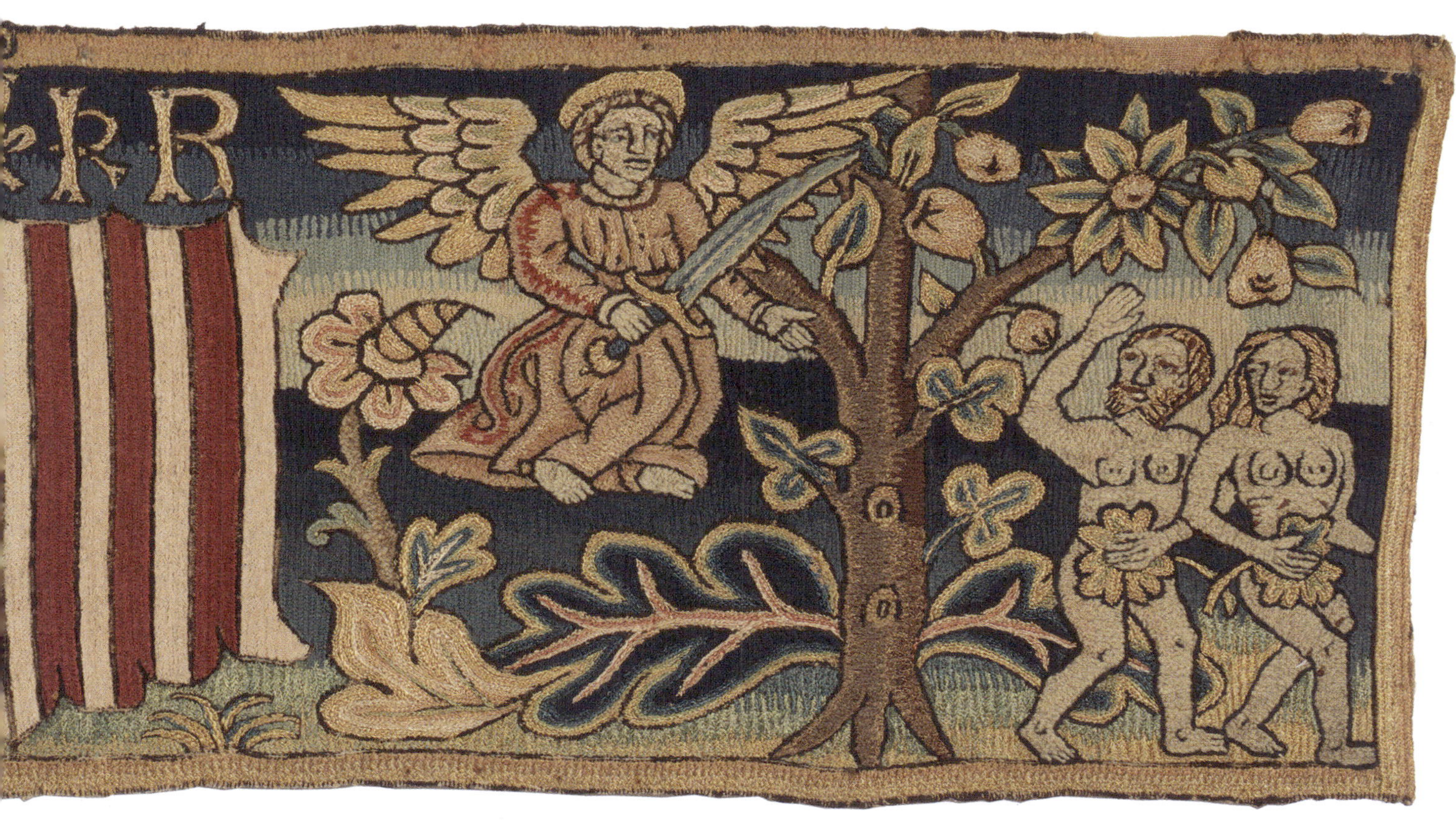

Valance, about 1550
Silk, linen
Made in Scotland
33 cm x 120 cm
29.181

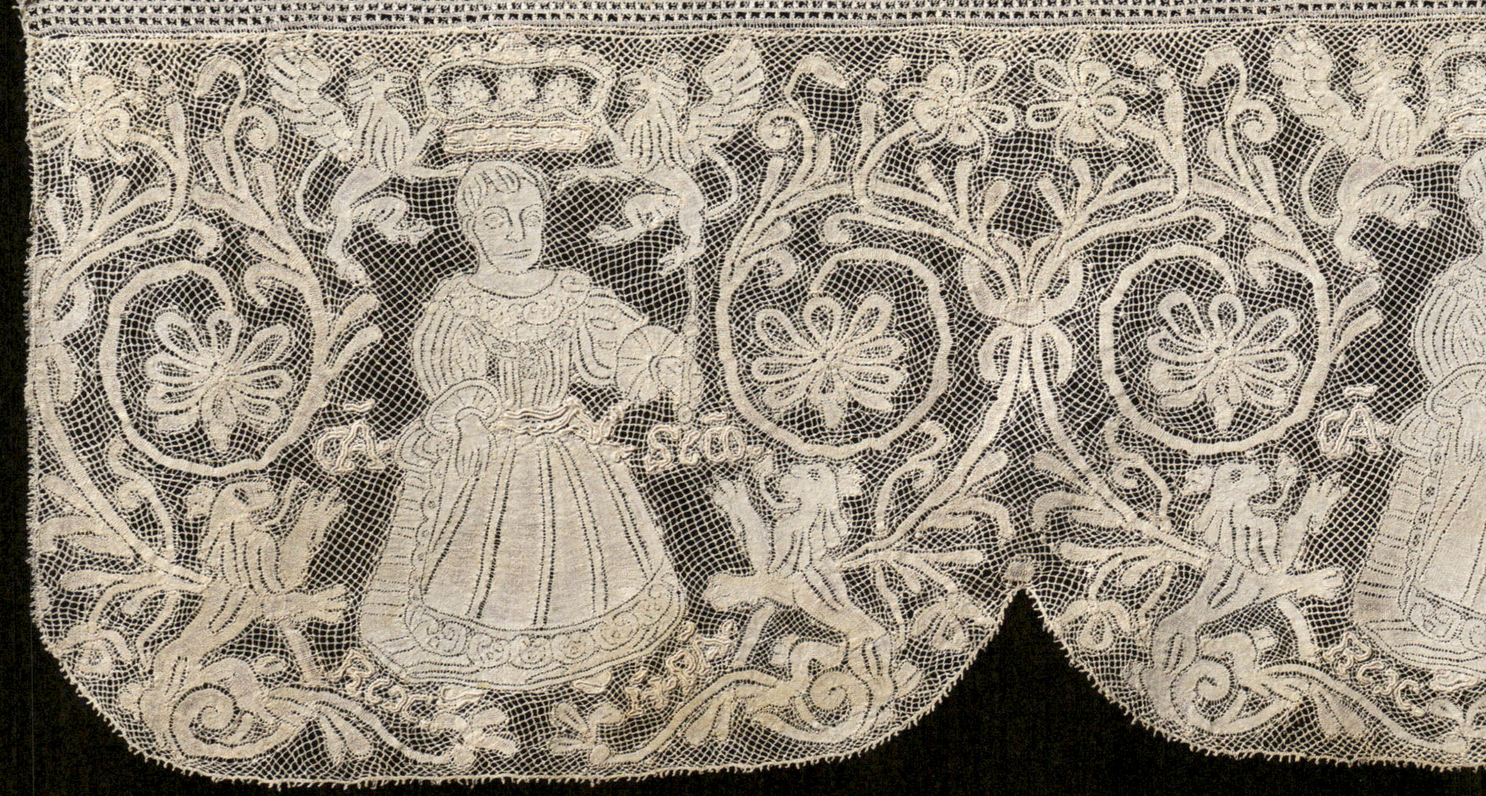

This lace border was made to celebrate the coronation of King Charles II of Spain (1661–1700) in 1665. Charles II was only four years old when he became king, and the lace features repeated motifs of the young monarch flanked by lions and with a crown above his head.

The Burrells collected 121 items of lace for the Collection. Constance Burrell had a particular interest in the lace and embroideries, purchasing objects herself to expand these areas. Her expert knowledge of lace meant that in 1956 she examined the lace for the Glasgow Corporation, leading to an increase in its valuation.

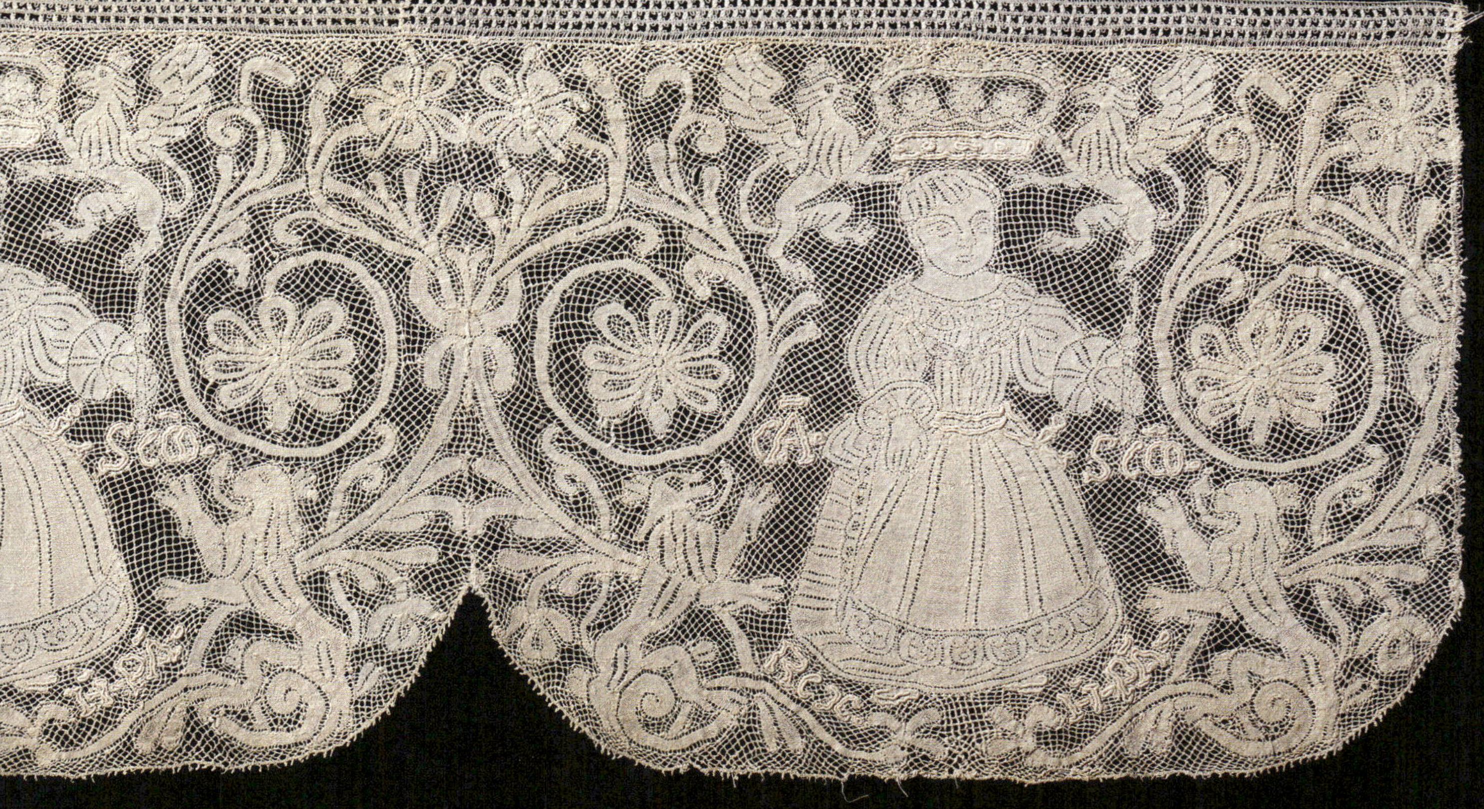

Lace border, 1665
Linen
Made in Spanish Netherlands, Flanders
19 cm x 67.5 cm
24.13

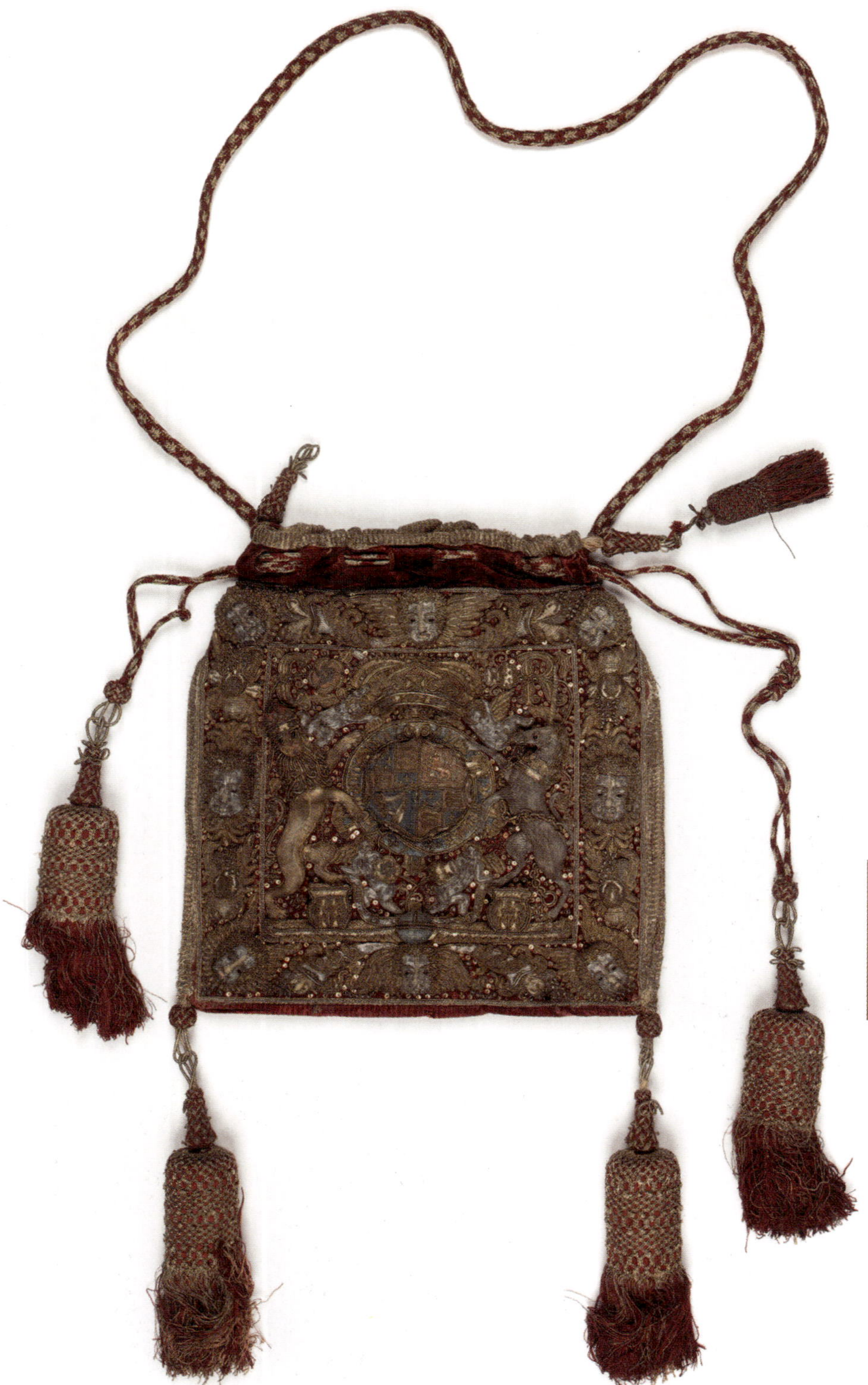

William Burrell acquired several embroidery and textile objects of royal regalia. This burse was made for Sir Francis North, 1st Baron Guilford (1637–85), who was appointed by King Charles II (1630–85) as Keeper of the Great Seal in 1682. The seal was held by the Keeper as a symbol of his authority over the law. It was kept in a ceremonial bag, a unique one being created for each newly appointed Keeper. This burse is ornately embroidered with blue and red silk, and silver and gilt threads, with the royal coat of arms of England, roses, thistles, and cherubs. The braided drawstring helped to close the bag.

Burse for the Great Seal of England,
about 1682–85
Silk, metal, wood
Made in England
43 cm x 40.5 cm
29.153

The Berwick Connection

The Burrell family had owned Hutton Castle since 1915, and took an active role in the development of nearby Berwick-upon-Tweed just over the border in England. In 1949 the Burrells donated 42 paintings to the town, establishing the Berwick Art Gallery. The Burrells also donated over 300 decorative art objects, including Chinese and Japanese porcelain, Venetian glass, and pewter.

Burrell himself carefully selected which paintings would be gifted to Berwick. The chosen works became a point of contention between Burrell and Dr Tom Honeyman, who wanted to retain two paintings, but the Burrells proceeded with the donation. Sir William Burrell spoke at the Berwick Art Gallery opening ceremony in May 1949, stating it gave him and Constance 'the greatest pleasure to bring those pictures together… to offer them to the ancient and honourable town of Berwick'.[5]

[5] 'Opening of Berwick's New Art Gallery: Gift of Sir William and Lady Burrell', *The Berwick Advertiser*, Thursday 12 May 1949, Issue No: 7341, p.7, 29 April 2021.

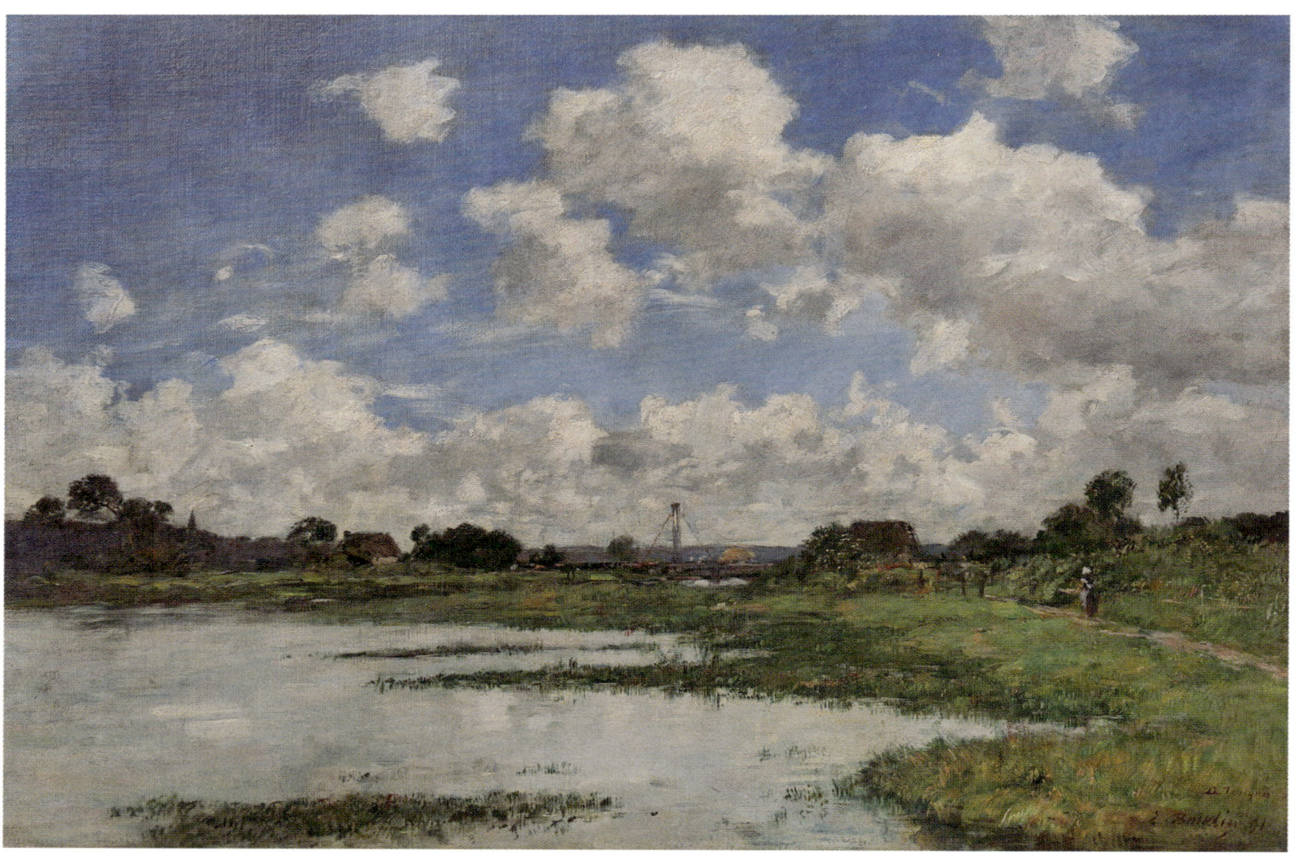

The Burrell Collection holds 11 works by French Impressionist painter Eugène Boudin (1824–98). This includes two paintings showing washerwomen working by the banks of the River Touques, in Normandy. The landscape shown here, which Burrell gifted to Berwick as part of the 1949 donation, shows Boudin's love for painting water, sky, and landscape; the blue sky with large clouds is reflected in the river water below, framed by luscious green riverbanks on which a small figure, possibly a washerwoman, wanders along the riverside.

River Touques, 1891
Eugène Louis Boudin
Oil on canvas
66 cm x 88.5 cm
Berwick Museum and Art Gallery (Museums Northumberland)
BERMG 1425

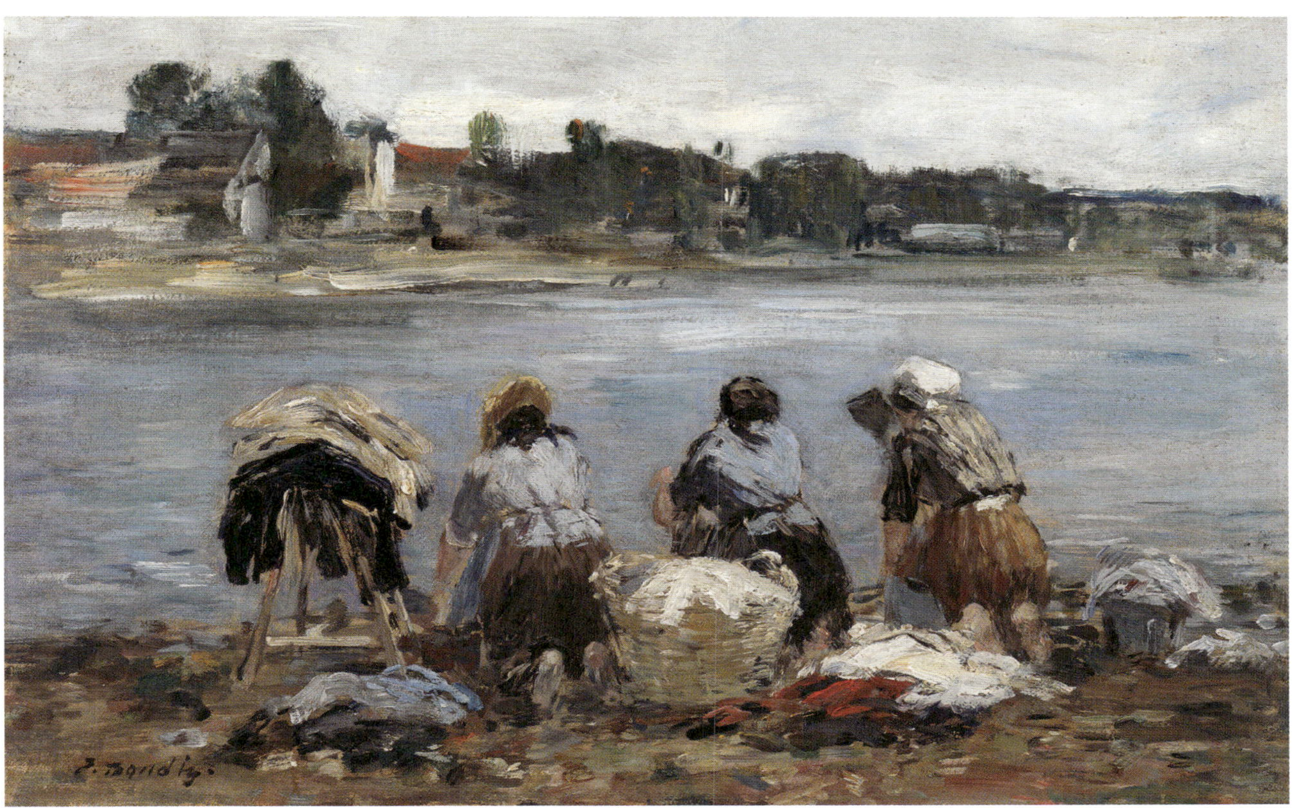

Boudin's paintings of the River Touques allowed him to combine his interest in painting human figures amongst the power of colourful landscapes. This painting shows three local women, seen from behind, busily chatting and surrounded by bundles of clothes which they scrub and soak in the river water.

Washerwomen on the Banks of the River Touques,
about 1888–95
Eugène Boudin
Oil on panel
20.6 cm x 33 cm
35.50

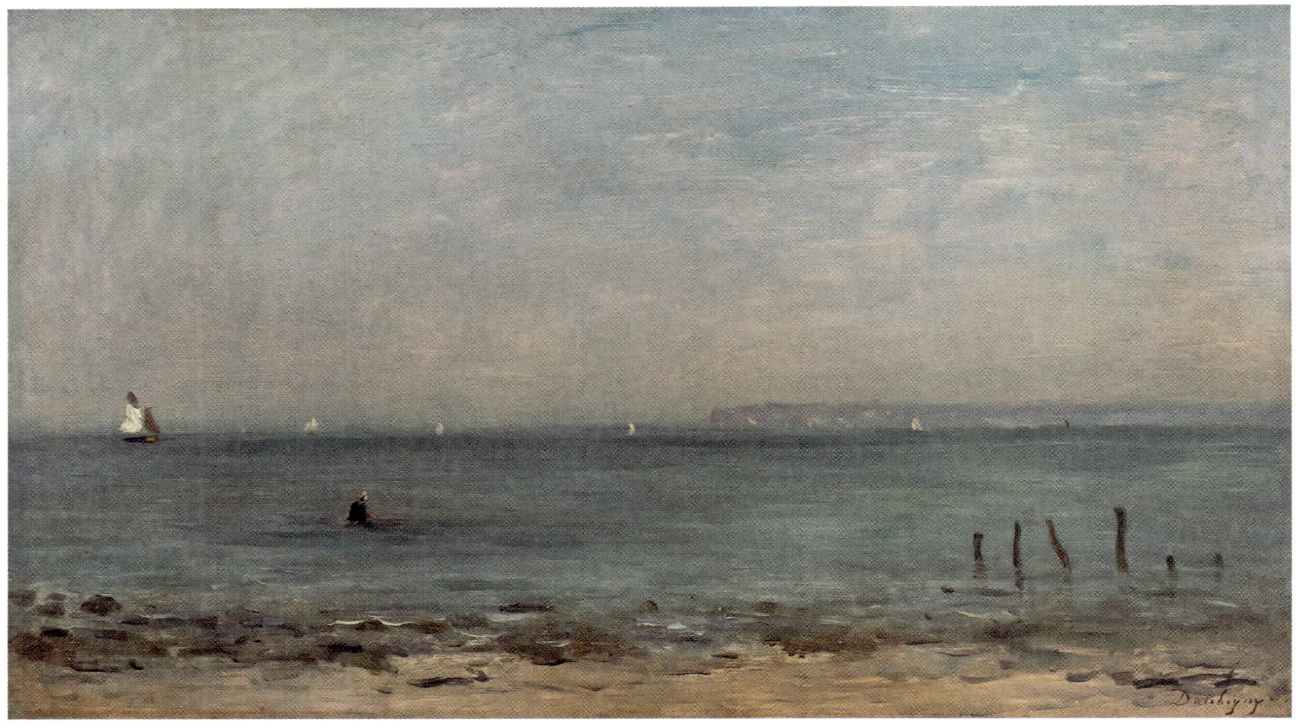

As part of the 1949 Berwick donation, William Burrell decided to gift this beach scene by French artist, Charles-François Daubigny (1817–78). The director of the Glasgow Art Galleries, Dr Tom Honeyman, immediately contacted Burrell to dissuade him, writing '…it would be lamentable if the finest example of his work were taken from the Burrell Collection.'[6] Much to Honeyman's dismay, William Burrell stood firm on his decision, and the Daubigny went to Berwick.

Beach at Villerville (Cap Gris Nez), 1870
Charles-François Daubigny
Oil on panel
51.4 cm x 74.2 cm
Berwick Museum and Art Gallery (Museums Northumberland)
BERMG 1431

[6] Richard Marks, *Burrell: A Portrait of a Collector*, Richard Drew Publishing (1988), p.163.

William Burrell bought 30 colourful Japanese woodcut prints during his lifetime. Woodcut prints were produced in their thousands in Japan during the 1600s, 1700s, and 1800s. This print shows Shoki, the Demon Queller, a religious figure of Chinese origin adopted into Japanese mythology. Shoki was the King of Ghosts, charged with hunting spirits that escaped Hell. With a wild mass of black hair, thunderous expression and brandishing a sharp sword, Shoki has caught an escaped demon, known as an *oni*, holding them tight under his arm. Despite the *oni's* sharp claws, it is trapped in Shoki's grasp, soon to be taken back to Hell.

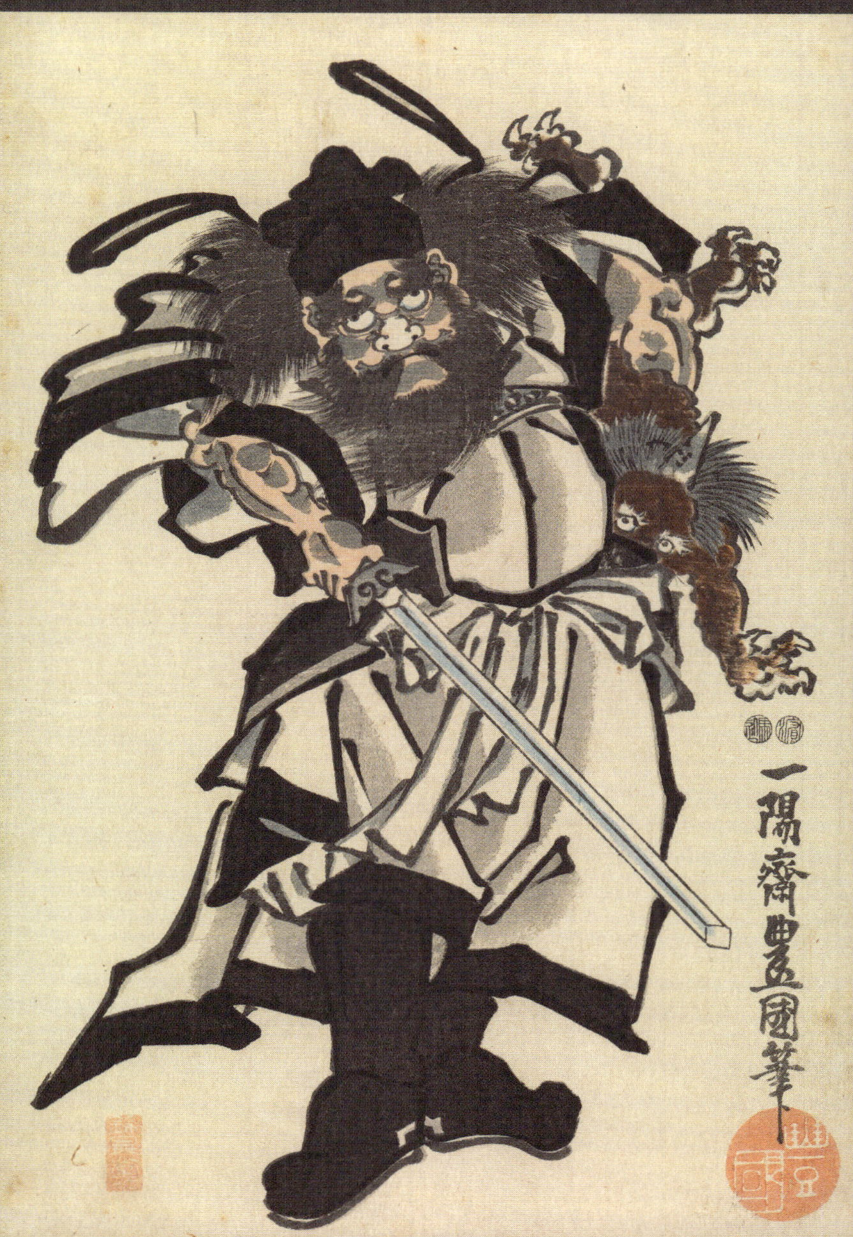

Shoki the Demon Queller, 1849–53
Utagawa Kunisada
Paper, ink
Made in Japan
35.8 cm x 24.1 cm
37.4

The Burrells gave Berwick several examples of Japanese Imari ware porcelain, also known as Arita ware. It was made in the areas surrounding the town of Arita in southern Japan. By the late 1600s Arita ware was mainly produced for export to Europe, shipped from the port of Imari. Imari porcelain is characterized by its use of bright blue, red, and black glazes, as seen on this pair of porcelain geisha figures.

In the early 1700s pink glazes were introduced, shown on the porcelain plate opposite donated by the Burrells. The plate features popular motifs and busy patterns of flowers, landscapes, and animals. The addition of gilding creating a golden effect on the porcelain was introduced to directly appeal to European tastes.

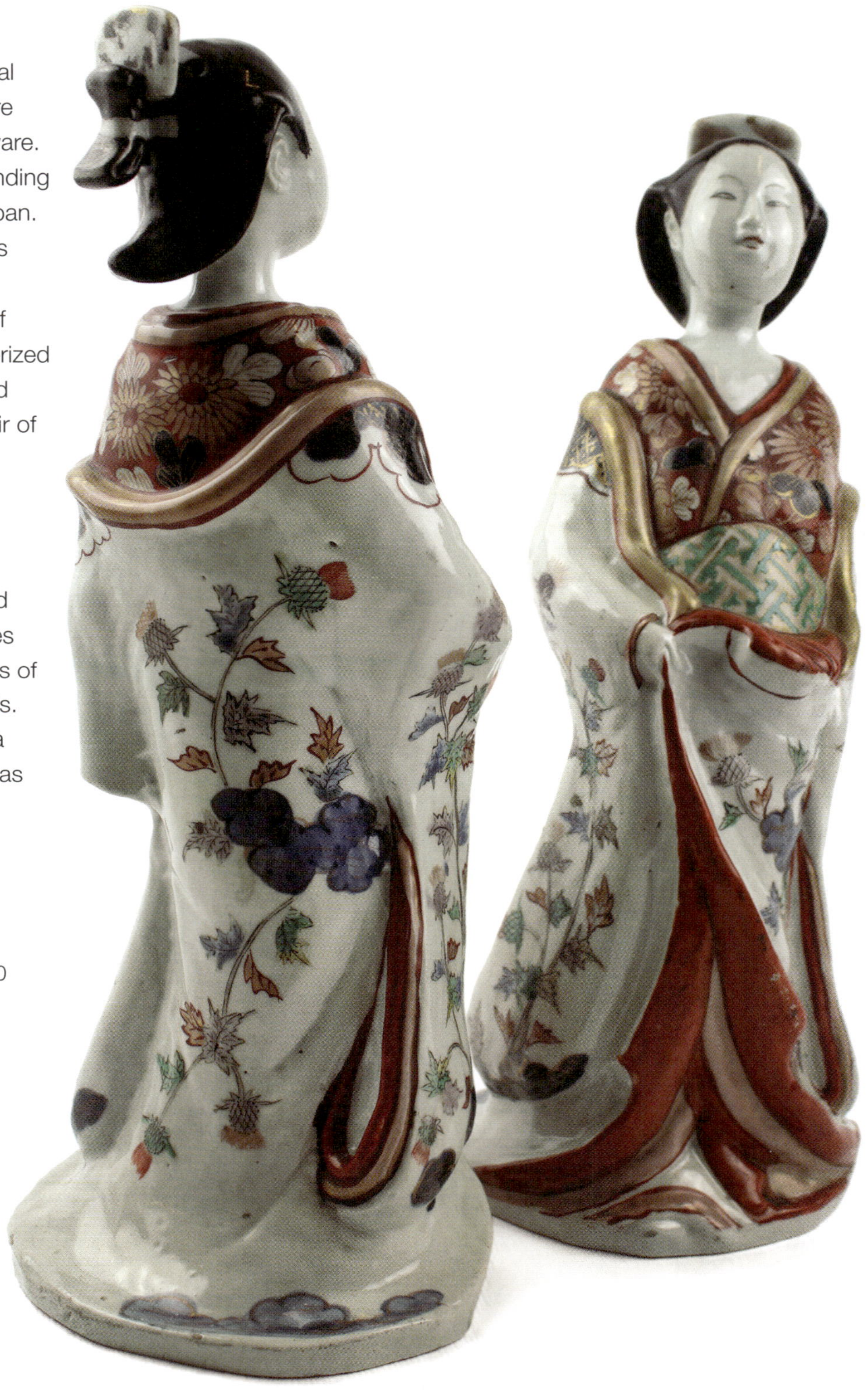

Pair of geisha figures, 1700–1800
Porcelain
Made in Japan
35.5.cm, 36 cm
Berwick Museum and Art Gallery
(Museums Northumberland)
BERMG 198 & 199

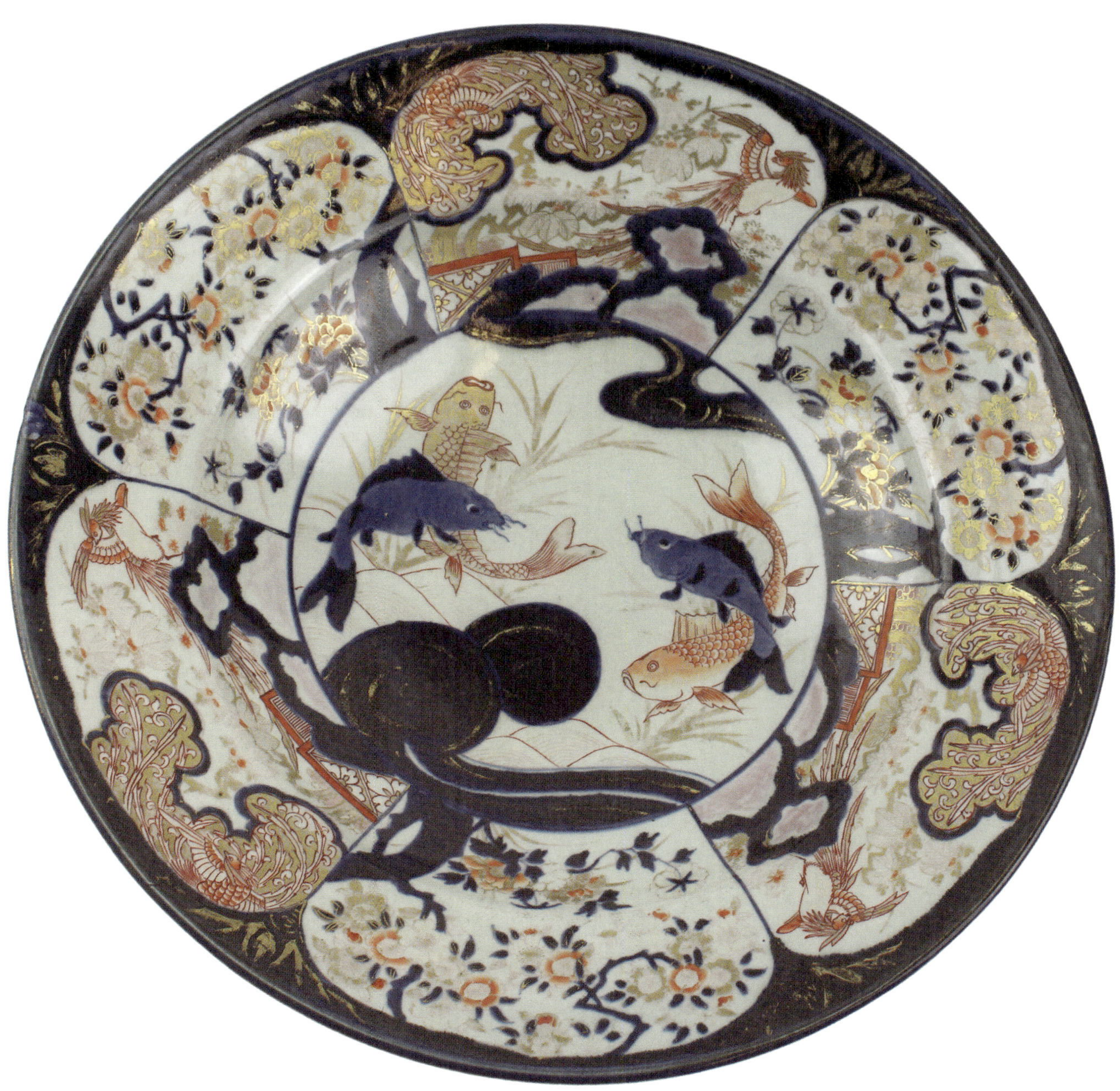

Dish with carp and chrysanthemum, 1700–1800
Porcelain
Made in Japan
Diameter: 54.5 cm
Berwick Museum and Art Gallery (Museums Northumberland)
BERMG 262

Mirror with tortoise and crane, 1800–1900
Bronze
Made in Japan
Berwick Museum and Art Gallery
(Museums Northumberland)
BERMG 563

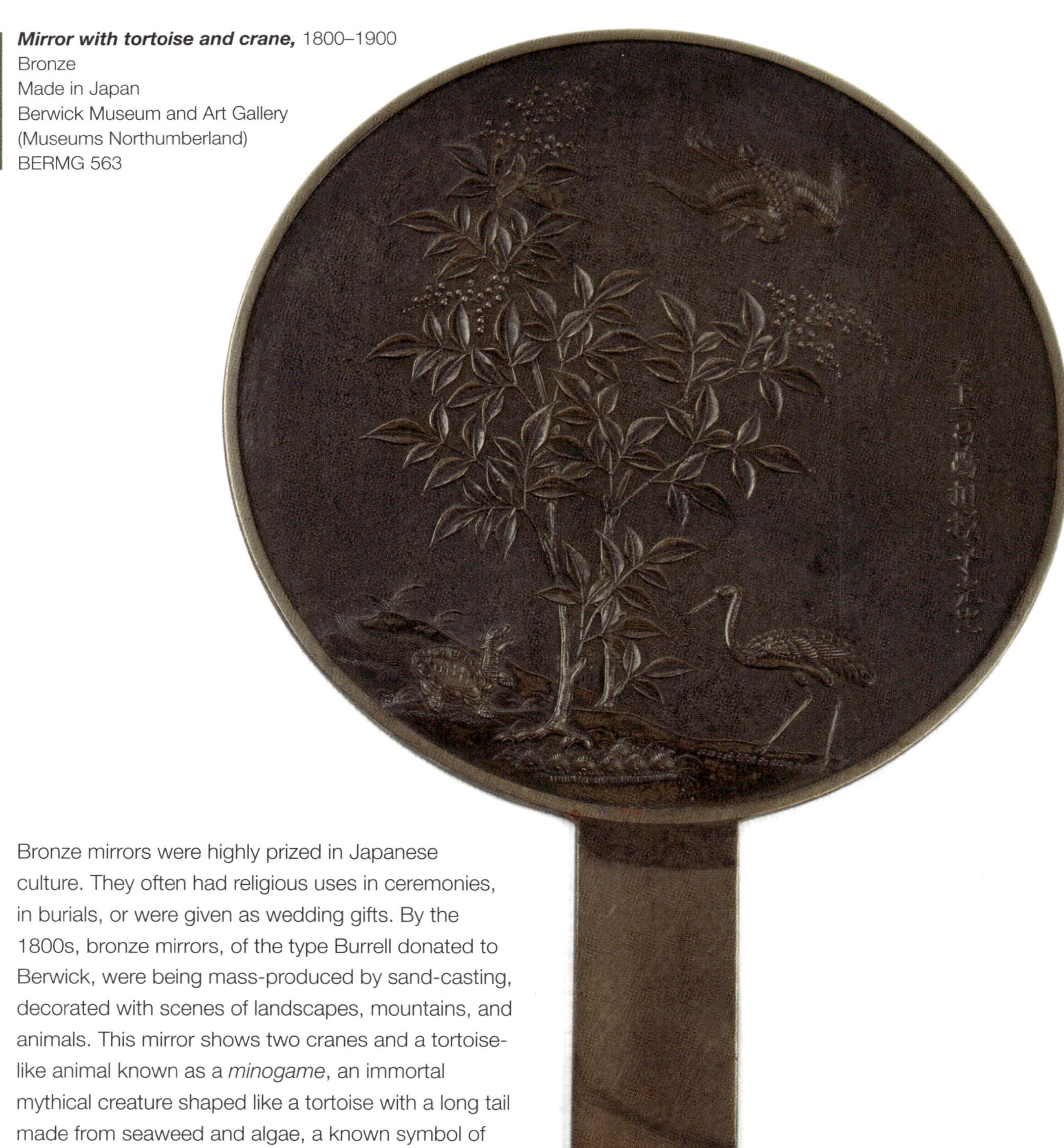

Bronze mirrors were highly prized in Japanese culture. They often had religious uses in ceremonies, in burials, or were given as wedding gifts. By the 1800s, bronze mirrors, of the type Burrell donated to Berwick, were being mass-produced by sand-casting, decorated with scenes of landscapes, mountains, and animals. This mirror shows two cranes and a tortoise-like animal known as a _minogame_, an immortal mythical creature shaped like a tortoise with a long tail made from seaweed and algae, a known symbol of long life and happiness.

From Collector to Corporation

During the early 1950s, many locations were scoped and suggested for the site of the future Burrell Collection museum. These included Mugdock Castle and the Douglaston estate, both near Milngavie to the north of Glasgow; however, plans for these locations fell through.[7] The setbacks in finding a home for the Collection unfortunately meant that Sir William Burrell would not live to see the new museum building. After devoting nearly 75 years of his life to his collection, he died at Hutton Castle on 29 March 1958, aged 96. Constance Burrell's death followed on 15 August 1961.

The perfect home for the Collection arrived nine years after Burrell's death, when in 1967 Dame Anne Maxwell Macdonald (1906–2011), owner of Pollok House and Estate, gifted the house and lands to the City of Glasgow. Set far enough outside the air pollution of the city centre, the large 'picnic field' near the middle of the park was chosen as the new site for the museum.

In September 1970 an architectural competition was launched to find a design for the Burrell Collection. The Competition Pack sent to all applicants gave an overview of the requirements for the building, and details of objects and architectural fragments to be displayed and incorporated into it. The Burrells had requested that the Collection 'as far as possible be shown as it would be in a private house … placed in rooms through the building with appropriate furniture so as to ensure … little resemblance to a Museum as possible.'[8] This desired interior scheme also had to be carefully considered by competition entrants.

The competition received 242 entries, with the winning design created by architects Barry Gasson, Brit Andresen, and John Meunier. Barry Gasson reflected that 'this was to be a Collection in a park, not in a city'[9]. Taking inspiration from the natural park setting, they designed a building that brought collection and parklands together in a complementary aesthetic. The inclusion of a glass wall along the north side of the building allowed the Collection to have the intimate and natural backdrop of the Pollok woodlands and the changing seasons. Gasson Architects also created distinct central interior spaces away from the glass exteriors for the hanging of tapestries and other objects that required protection from natural light. The building design included storage for the complete collection, a restaurant, library, office spaces, conservation workshops, photography studios, and a plant room, making the building a functional museum space that met the needs of both staff and visitors. Work began on the site on 4 May 1978, with the Burrells' daughter, Silvia, pushing the button to start the first bulldozer on the picnic field.

On 21 October 1983 the Burrell Collection was officially opened by Queen Elizabeth II, and within the first year received over one million visitors. Finally, 39 years after its initial donation, the Collection had a permanent home where the people of Glasgow could marvel over the great gift of Sir William Burrell and Constance, Lady Burrell.

[7] Richard Marks, *Burrell: A Portrait of a Collector*, Richard Drew Publishing (1988), p.167–169.

[8] Richard Marks, *Burrell: A Portrait of a Collector*, Richard Drew Publishing (1988), p.156.

[9] Barry Gasson, 'Notes on the Building' in *The Burrell Collection*, Collins London and Glasgow in association with Glasgow Museums and Art Galleries, 1983, p.15.

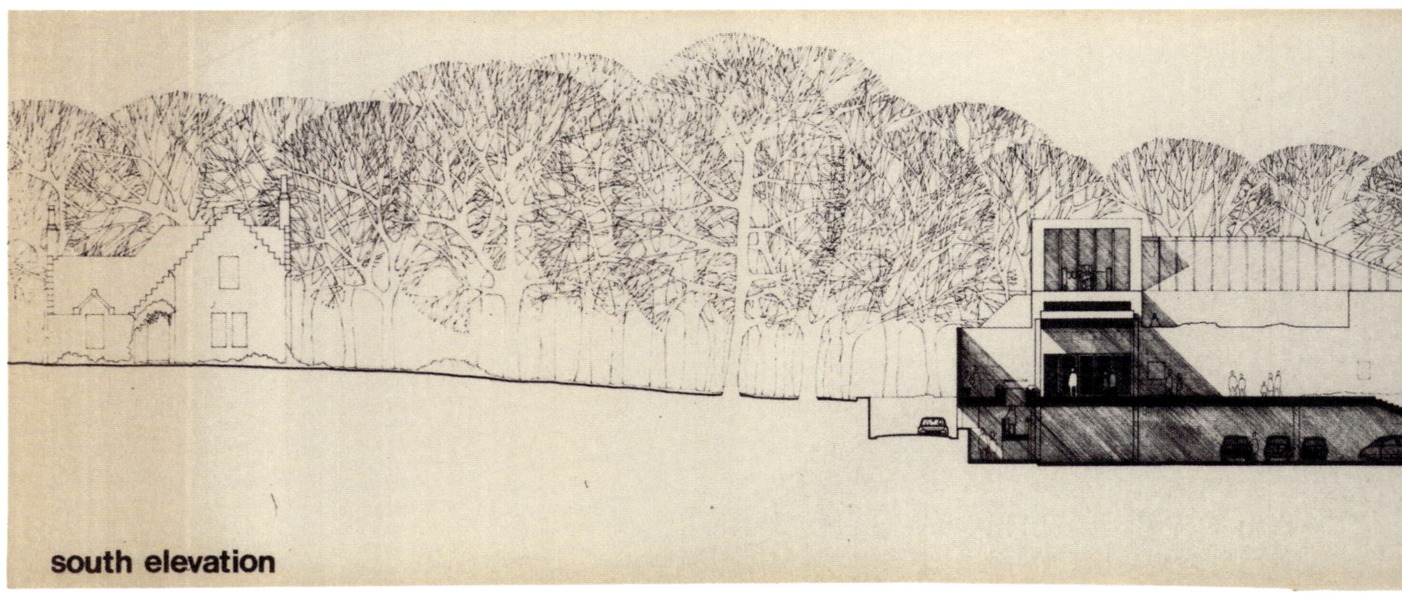

This architectural drawing shows an elevation of the south side of the building. Gasson added tiny details to the drawing to give the sense of the working functions of the museum. Figures of people are seen wandering the galleries and eating in the basement restaurant. The main feature of the south wall was the hanging of the stained glass along the glass exterior, allowing natural light to pour through. Gasson has drawn the stained-glass panels in the elevation, supported by timber framing.

Drawing of Burrell Collection south elevation,
about 1972–75
Barry Gasson Architects
Paper, ink
16.8 cm x 81.4 cm
GMA.2013.1.3.47

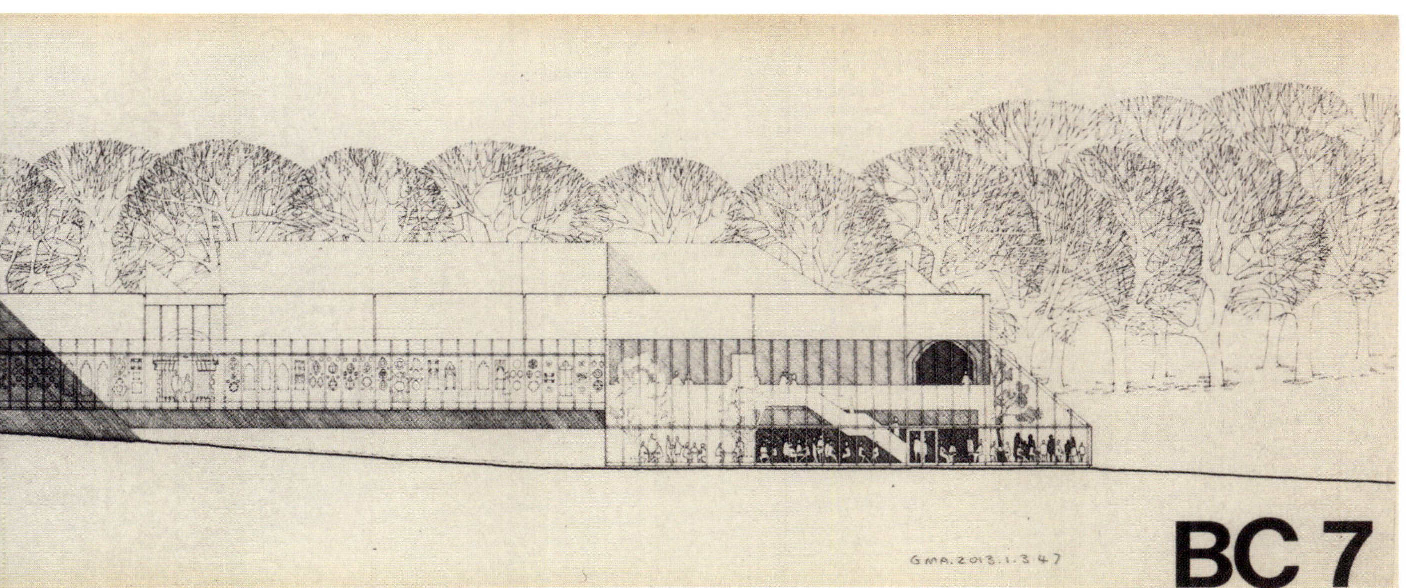

This drawing shows Gasson's designs for the erection of the Hornby Castle Portal in the museum courtyard. The portal was once the main entrance to Hornby Castle's hall, in Yorkshire. It was purchased in 1953 from the collection of American newspaper magnate, William Randolph Hearst (1861–1951), as part of four lots of architectural fragments to be incorporated into the new museum. The architects searched for the original quarry from which the limestone for the portal was sourced, in order to create a supporting structure for the fragment using the same limestone. However, upon finding the quarry was no longer active, they opted for distinctive pink sandstone which can still be seen in the courtyard today.[10]

Drawing of Hornby Portal, about 1972–75
Barry Gasson Architects
Paper, ink
76 cm x 59.6 cm
GMA.2013.1.3.1385

[10] Barry Gasson, 'Notes on the Building' in *The Burrell Collection*, Collins London and Glasgow in association with Glasgow Museums and Art Galleries, 1983, p.16.

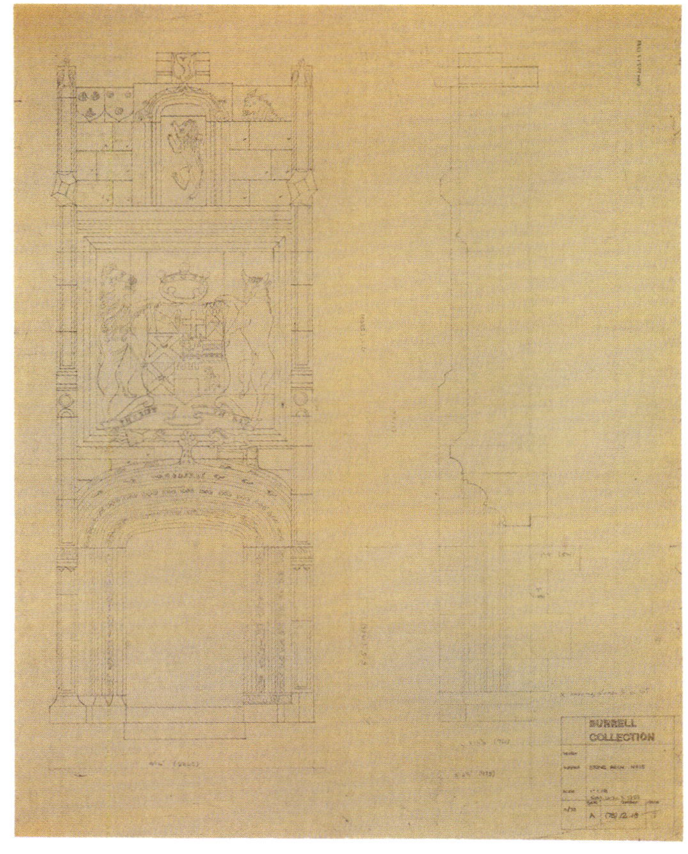

Cabinet, about 1640–1700
Ebony, silk, brass
Made in Antwerp, Belgium
44.4 cm x 49.1 cm x 30.1 cm
14.433

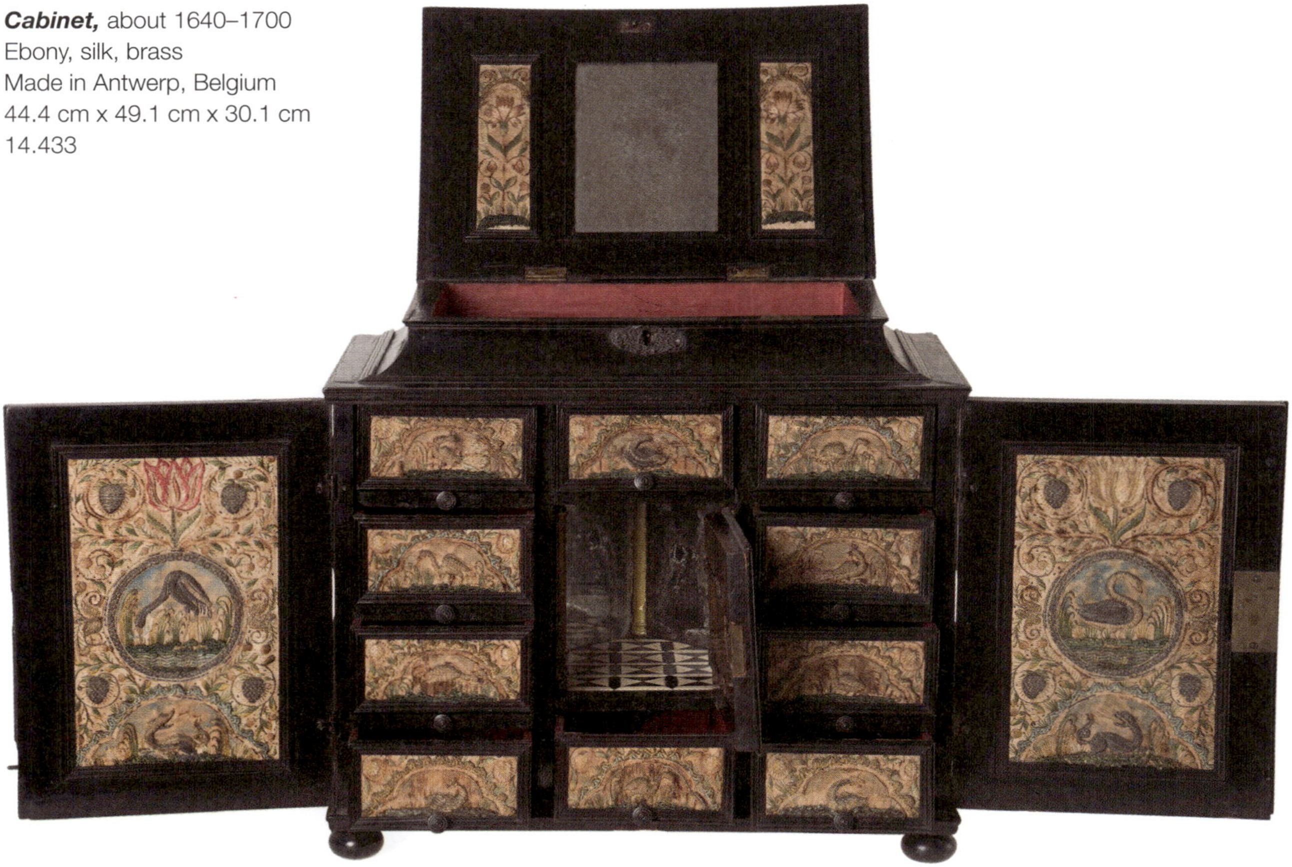

The purchase of this cabinet is not noted in any of
William Burrell's purchase books, suggesting it was
bought before he started recording his objects in
1911. During the 1600s Antwerp was the centre of
manufacture for ebony cabinets. Produced for export,
cabinets were used to display private collections of
'curiosities', coins, medals, natural history specimens,
and antiquities. The external doors of this cabinet
open to reveal a series of small drawers with silk
embroidery panels decorated with birds, animals,
and flowers. Behind the central door is a miniature
space, known as a *perspective*, with mirrored walls
and black and white tiled floor. The perspective would
display the most important 'curiosity', with the mirrors
reflecting the object from all angles.

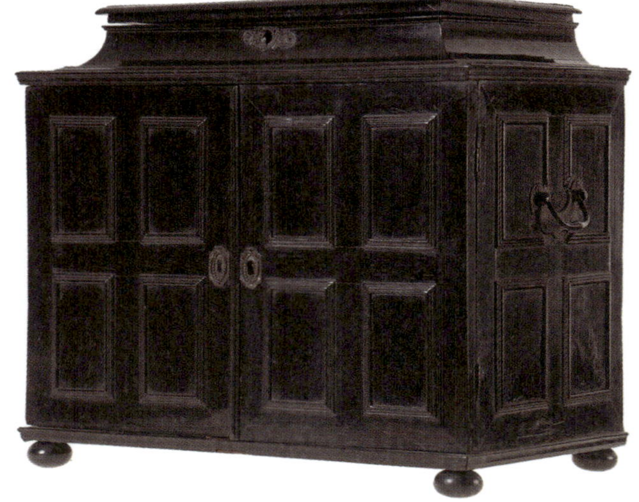

Sir William Burrell bought this rare Elizabethan table in 1946. The tabletop is decorated with inlaid coloured woods making decorative strapwork patterns entwined with motifs of flowers, animals, birds, figures and heraldic shields with the coat of arms of the Brome and Crossley families. This table was most likely made to celebrate a marriage between members of the two families, the inlaid decorations of the initials 'IB' and 'MB' with the date '1569' probably commemorating the names of the married couple and the date they wed.

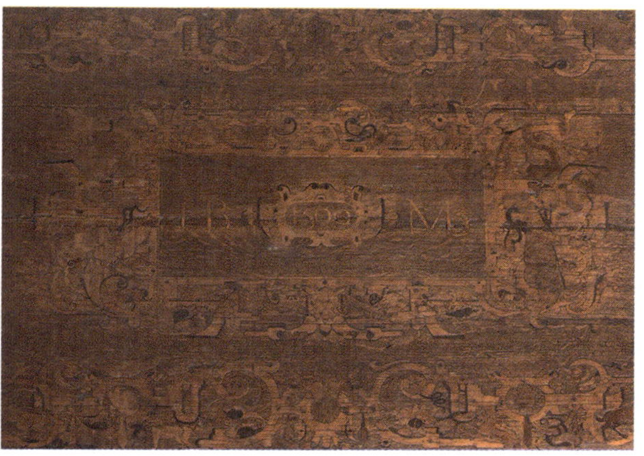

Table, known as the 'Brome table', 1569
Oak
Made in England
90 cm x 229.5 cm x 102.3 cm
14.306

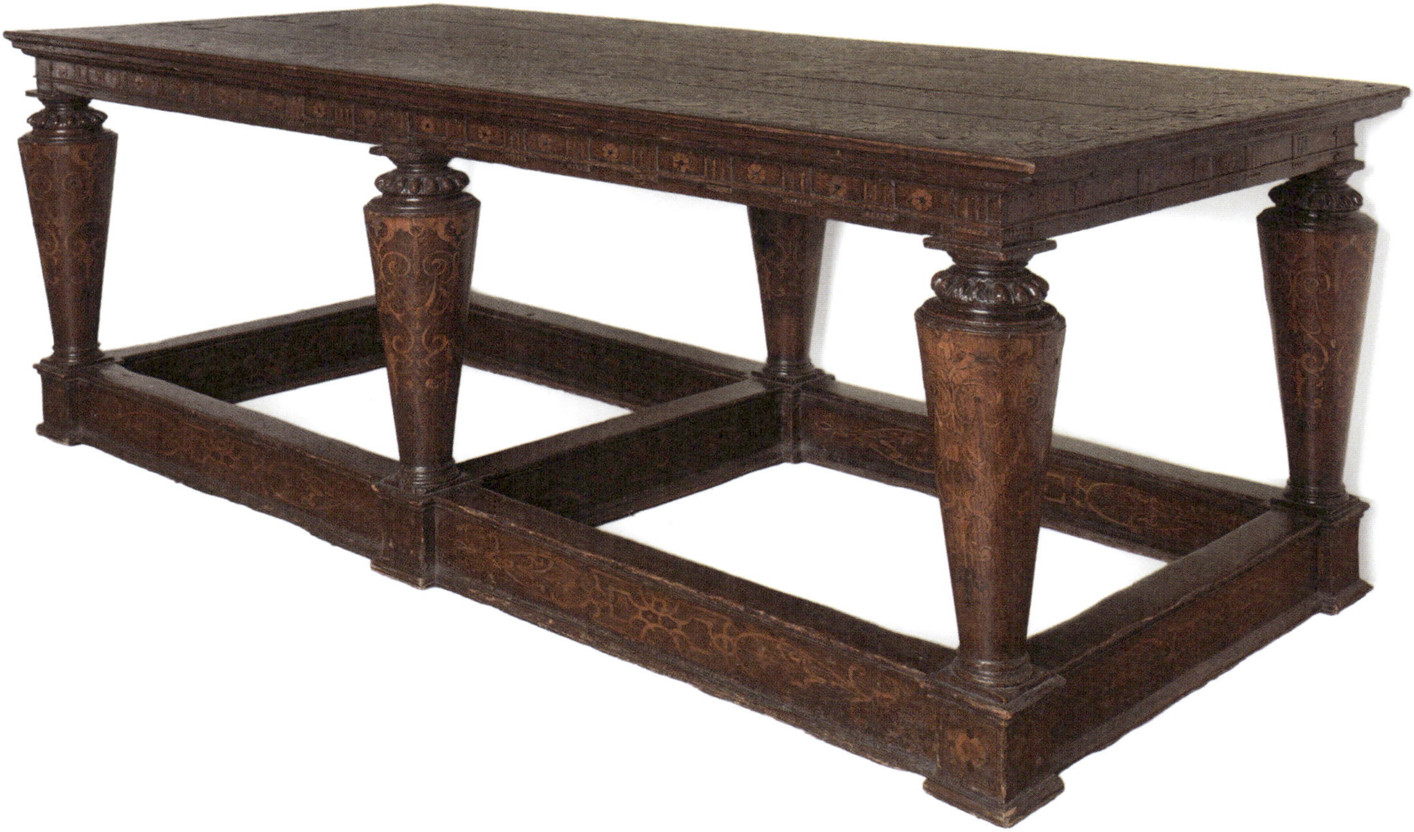

Sir William Burrell collected a wide range
of large pile carpets from the Middle East,
Central Asia, and Northern India. Most were
used in his home, Hutton Castle, to furnish
the floors, but as museum objects became
some of the largest items to find space for in
the new museum building.

Burrell bought this carpet in 1940 for
£3,000, believing it to have been a gift
from the Shah of Persia to Empress Maria
Theresa (1717–80). The central medallion
is decorated with an ivory arabesque scroll
with multi-coloured flowers joined by a
network of blue stems. The centre field is
crammed with rows of large palmettes with
sharpened edges, giving a flame-like effect.

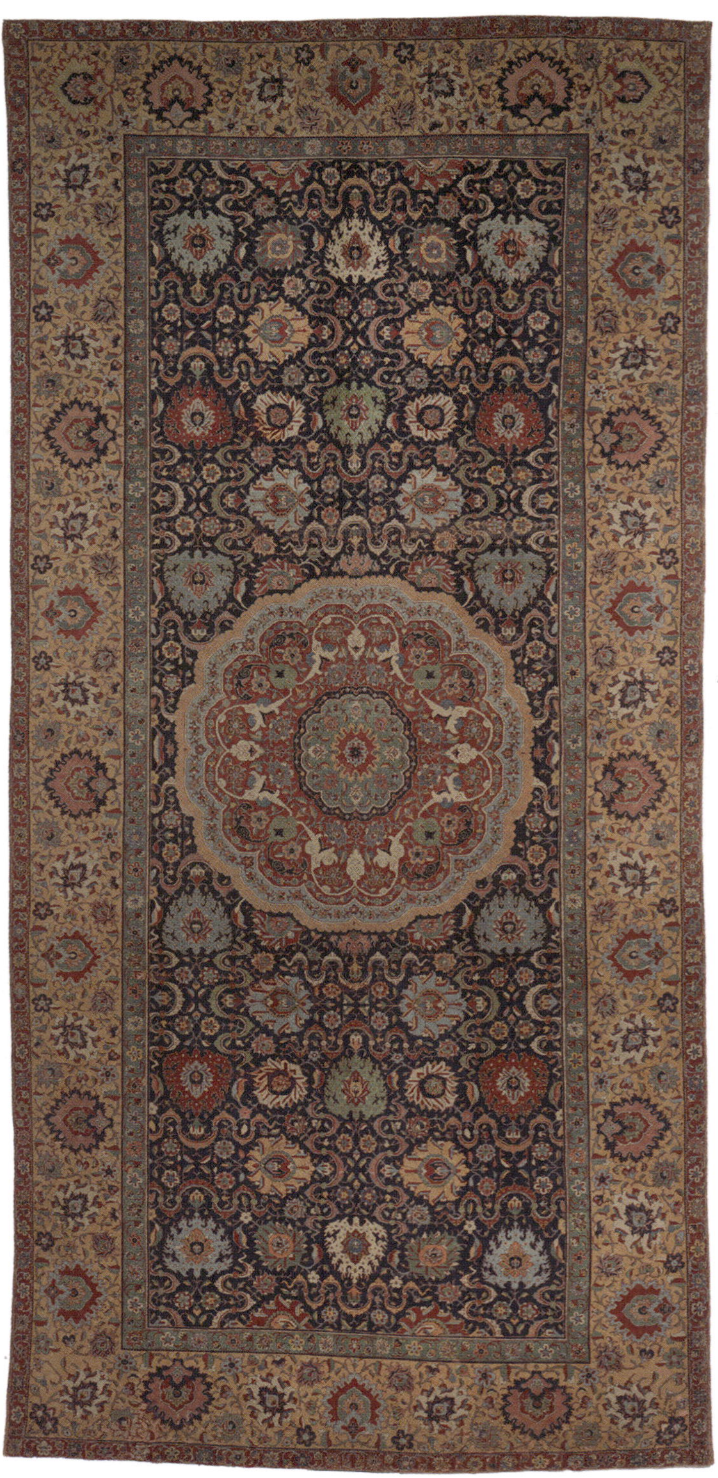

The Dietrichstein Carpet, 1700–1850
Safavid Period (possibly Qajar)
Cotton warp and weft, wool pile
Made in Tabriz, Iran
487.7 cm x 223.5 cm
9.37